Warrior • 75

Comanche 1800–74

Douglas V Meed • Illustrated by Jonathan Smith

First published in Great Britain in 2003 by Osprey Publishing,
Elms Court, Chapel Way, Botley, Oxford OX2 9LP, United Kingdom.
Email: info@ospreypublishing.com

A CIP catalog record for this book is available from the British Library

ISBN 1 84176 587 2

Douglas V. Meed has asserted his right under the Copyright, Designs and
Patents Act, 1988, to be identified as the Author of this Work.

Editor: Gerard Barker
Design: Ken Vail Graphic Design, Cambridge, UK
Index by Alan Thatcher
Originated by The Electronic Page Company, Cwmbran, UK
Printed in China through World Print Ltd.

03 04 05 06 07   10 9 8 7 6 5 4 3 2 1

FOR A CATALOGUE OF ALL BOOKS PUBLISHED BY OSPREY MILITARY AND
AVIATION PLEASE CONTACT:

The Marketing Manager, Osprey Direct UK, PO Box 140,
Wellingborough, Northants, NN8 2FA, United Kingdom.
Email: info@ospreydirect.co.uk

The Marketing Manager, Osprey Direct USA,
c/o MBI Publishing, PO Box 1, 729 Prospect Ave,
Osceola, WI 54020, USA.
Email: info@ospreydirectusa.com

Buy online at **www.ospreypublishing.com**

Artist's note

Readers may care to note that the original paintings from
which the color plates in this book were prepared are
available for private sale. All reproduction copyright
whatsoever is retained by the Publishers. All enquiries
should be addressed to:

Jonathan Smith
107 Ryeworth Road
Cheltenham
Gloucester
GL52 6LS
UK

The Publishers regret that they can enter into no
correspondence upon this matter.

CONTENTS

COMANCHE 1800–74

INTRODUCTION

History first records the Comanches in the 17th century, when they were part of the Shoshoni tribes that roamed the mountain forests in the upper reaches of the Platte River in what is now eastern Wyoming. On foot, the men trapped small animals and with difficulty hunted stray buffalo with stone-tipped spears and war clubs. The women gathered berries and nuts to supplement the meager diet. The Comanches fought with marginal success against neighboring tribes over hunting grounds and waterholes and were often viewed with contempt by the more organized tribes of the Crow, Blackfoot, and Apaches.

During the late 17th century, Comanche bands descended onto the Southern Plains, which stretch north to south for almost 700 miles (1,100km) from Kansas down to the beginnings of the hill country of central Texas, and from east to west some 400 miles (650km) from the forests of east Texas into eastern New Mexico. At this time, this vast region was inhabited by only a few scattered nomadic tribes, as well as millions of American buffalo that grazed the lush grasslands. It was here that the Comanches learned to capture, ride, and domesticate the wild descendants of horses that had escaped from Spanish Conquistadores who had probed into New Mexico in the 16th century. By 1700 the horse had revolutionized the Comanche way of life.

From short, often bandy-legged and footsore scavengers, the Comanches became the most skilled horsemen in North America. Their courage, daring, and ruthlessness soon made them the most feared of all the nomadic tribes that followed the massive buffalo herds across the American heartland.

They referred to themselves as "Our People" but rival tribes began to use the term "Comanche," a corruption of an Indian word meaning, "those who are against us", or simply "enemy." The name stuck.

During the years before they descended onto the Southern Plains, the Comanches were shunned by other mountain tribes because of their ferocity. Here, Comanche warriors are attacking Utes who ventured onto their hunting grounds. (Denver Public Library)

For more than 150 years Comanche warriors were the "Lords of the Southern Plains." They drove out competing tribes and were a fighting barrier to American settlement. Raiding beyond the borders of Comancheria they raised havoc from Kansas to deep into Mexico. (Meed Collection)

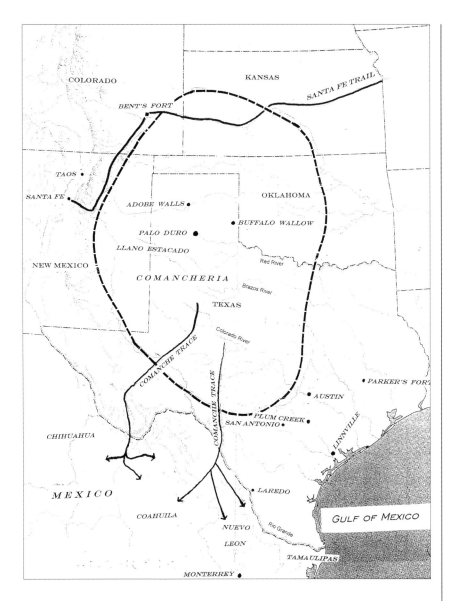

For more than 150 years mounted Comanche warriors were "the lords of the Southern Plains." Their ferocious raids struck terror into the hearts of other Plains tribes, Mexican villagers, and the American settlers of frontier Texas. Comanche horsemen ranged over the vast area known as Comancheria, and they raided over an area that stretched from southern Colorado and Kansas to northern Mexico.

The tribe was divided into 12 different clans which usually united only for war. Trailing the buffalo herds for most of the year, the Comanches operated in small independent bands rarely numbering more than 100 men, women, and children. The total number of Comanches at the peak of their supremacy is widely estimated at more than 20,000, but that figure is little more than a guess.

During winter, Comanche bands huddled along streams in semi-permanent camps; warriors stuck close to home. In late spring, when the prairie grasses began to sprout and the shaggy horses shed their winter coats, the Comanche braves prepared to go out raiding.

5

Before they acquired horses, the Comanches stalked buffalo on foot. Here, hunters disguised as white wolves creep up within bow range of the herd. (Denver Public Library)

CHRONOLOGY 1700–1875

*c.*1700	Comanches descend onto the Southern Plains and adopt the horse culture
1709	Comanches begin to trade with New Mexico
1795	Comanche and Kiowa tribes form an alliance
*c.*1800	Comanches dominate Southern Plains
1831	Comancheros begin gun-running on a large scale
1836	May – Comanches attack Fort Parker
1840	March 19 – Council House Fight in San Antonio
	August 12 – Battle of Plum Creek
1854	Comanche reservation established on Clear Fork of Brazos River, Texas
1859	Comanches expelled from Texas, trek to Oklahoma reservation
1861–65	Raids on Texas settlements increase during the American Civil War
1867	Medicine Lodge Treaty signed. It fails to stop Comanche raids on Texas
1874	June 27 – Battle of Adobe Walls
	September 27/28 – Final battle at Palo Duro Canyon
1875	Quanah Parker surrenders at Fort Sill. All Comanches confined to reservation

LIFE ON THE PLAINS

By 1700, the tribe had reached the point of highest development of its horse and buffalo culture. Virtually everything the Comanches used or ate came from the buffalo. A full-grown bull buffalo was 7 feet (2m) high at the shoulder and weighed almost half a ton. The hides from these giants provided the material used to make tepees and bags for carrying water or other supplies; with the fur still on, the hides were put to use as heavy robes that could withstand the freezing winds that blew down the prairies in the winter months. Buffalo sinews were made into bowstrings; buffalo hooves were boiled to make glue.

And, of course, the buffalo was a source of meat. Noah Smithwick, a pioneer who alternately lived with, traded with, and fought against the Comanches, wrote that the tribe subsisted almost entirely on buffalo meat. The Comanches were, Smithwick wrote, "very fond of tripe, which they boiled without washing it, merely dragging it over the grass to wipe off the thickest of the filth." They also drank "curdled milk taken from the stomachs of suckling fawns and buffalo calves, which they esteemed a rare delicacy." Smithwick also added that the Comanches refused to drink the frontier whiskey that was often offered in trade by the Spaniards, Mexicans, and Texans.

Tasks were divided between men and women. Women gathered plant food, reared the children, and cooked. They also carried out the laborious task of pounding deer or buffalo hides to make them softer and more malleable.

Men rode out to hunt. After scouts located a buffalo herd, the hunting band circled downwind to approach the grazing beasts. Then whooping and hollering, they charged upon the herd, killing the buffalo with bow and arrow.

During warm months on the Plains, the men wore little more in camp than breechcloths of deer hide, although when riding they pulled on thigh-high deerskin leggings. The women wore dresses of doeskin, sometimes ornamented with colored trader's beads. Small boys ran naked about the camp, while girls usually wore a smaller version of their mother's dresses or skirts. In later years, the tribe traded for cotton or woolen clothes and an assortment of glass beads and metal trinkets for decorative purposes.

Comanche families were often polygamous, perhaps because the warrior's life, though glamorous, was often short. Marriages were conducted by parents with the suitor offering the girl's parents gifts of skins, assorted loot or, according to Smithwick, "If the girl was a belle," he would offer horses. Whatever their brutality to enemies and prisoners, a Comanche warrior would have felt disgraced to strike his wife.

Training

By 1800 the Comanche bands were at the peak of their power. They had bested the Osages, Utes, and Kiowas and had finally smashed Apache power on the Plains after decades of bitter fighting. They had intimidated the Pueblo tribes of central New Mexico, crushed Spanish

Unlike many other tribes, the Comanches did not honor aging warriors, such as Red Bird, shown here. When a warrior became too old or infirm to fight, he was scorned as a useless "old bull." (Denver Public Library)

Choppy, the wife of Paafybitty, wears a multi-colored trade-goods robe, and carries her baby in a cradle-board. When a woman gave birth, she gripped two stakes driven into the ground to support her while undergoing the pain of delivery. Many women died during childbirth. (Denver Public Library)

resistance, and established commercial relations with the Spanish-Mexican traders known as Comancheros, who were operating out of Santa Fe and Taos.

In this environment of Comanche mastery, our protagonist, a typical Comanche warrior, was born in 1800. Named Spotted Pony, he was a member of the Penateka clan of the southern Comanches. Since all male Comanches were destined to become warriors, the young boy began his training early in life.

Young boys were given small bows and arrows and soon learned to hunt small game. With blunt lances they learned to thrust and parry during mock battles fought with their playmates, who took turns pretending to be enemy tribesmen, the strange Spaniards in iron armor, or the dangerous Texan newcomers with their short guns that shot time after time.

To develop endurance Spotted Pony and the other boys ran foot races over the rough ground in the hot sun. Smithwick, who often raced with his Comanche friends, recounted that he could best them in a 50 yard (45m) dash. But because endurance was a cardinal virtue for a Comanche, boys always sprinted at least a quarter of a mile (400m), far enough to leave an exhausted Anglo lagging far behind.

Most importantly, the boys learned to ride their mustang horses almost as soon as they learned to walk. Games were a large part of equestrian training, and young boys learned to lasso turkeys, deer, wild mustangs, and buffalo calves while riding at the gallop.

Smithwick recounts that some of the games with which young tribesmen perfected their hunting skills were easily transformed into the stealthy and daring tactics they used in warfare. Concealed in brush, a young would-be warrior learned to wait patiently until a flock of turkeys broke cover and ventured into the open. Then he would ride down upon them, keeping his horse between them and the brush, chasing the flightless but fast-running birds until they were exhausted. Roping and then butchering them, he returned to camp to provide a turkey dinner for his family and glean some decorative turkey feathers for his hair, lance, or shield.

Young Spotted Pony undoubtedly practiced his archery by lurking near a waterhole. When a deer came to drink, he waited until the animal had had its fill. Then, when the deer's belly was filled and the now sluggish animal began to leave the waterhole, Spotted Pony let out a loud yell and rode swiftly to pursue the lumbering animal. Getting close, he loosed his arrows. When the animal dropped, it was quickly skinned to provide a soft dress for his mother or a sister. The whole family would then enjoy a supper of venison.

Spotted Pony also learned to covertly observe a waterhole until a wild mustang came to drink. When the beast was sluggish with a bellyful of water, the lad would pursue the horse at the gallop until he got close enough to lasso it. Kicking, squealing, and thrashing about, the mustang would be led back to camp to be trained to haul goods or gentled into a riding horse. The tamed animal would be added to its captor's remuda (herd of horses) or traded to a Comanchero for a steel knife, arrowheads, or a spear point, or perhaps to the parents of a pretty girl who would become his wife.

In the evening, after his all meat supper, Spotted Pony was allowed to sit in the tepee with the older warriors. There, smoking tobacco from wooden or stone pipes, the elders told tales of counting coup on enemy tribesmen, stealing horses from Mexican ranches, or scalping a white family who, unescorted, foolishly traveled across the Comancheria country that belonged to the tribe by way of conquest. The warriors were proud of the scars they carried from the horns of an enraged buffalo or the punctured flesh marks they received from an enemy lance blade, arrowhead, or bullet. Often they would outline their scar tissue with brightly colored ocher rings or with tattoos.

The nomadic Comanches traveled by horseback, the women riding with the men. Small children were bundled into a carrier which was strapped to the mother's back, an arrangement that kept the woman's hands free to control the horse or travois. (Denver Public Library)

It was from the warriors' tales that Spotted Pony and other young braves learned the arts of the hunt and the raid. When he reached adolescence and demonstrated that he could ride and shoot accurately with the bow, Spotted Pony was allowed to accompany the warriors on a buffalo hunt. After showing his daring by riding close to the horns of a rampaging bull buffalo and felling the beast with arrows, the young man returned to camp in new-found glory. He might then attach a buffalo tail to his shield.

The horse

The most potent weapon of the Comanche raiders was the mustang horse. On these swift steeds, endowed with great endurance, the Comanches could thunder down to surprise and kill buffalo, slaughter enemies, and rustle precious horses from unsuspecting settlers. The mustangs' speed also allowed the raiders to quickly scatter and escape from any pursuers.

Mustangs were usually not more than 5 feet (1.5m) high and weighed from 800 to 1,000lb (360–450kg). They were extremely hardy. In the natural horse country of the Plains, the mustangs had to endure

ABOVE **Life was hard for Comanche women. They did everything except hunt and fight. The nomadic life made child bearing difficult, and they were plagued by miscarriages and epidemics of European diseases. (George Catlin, 1836)**

RIGHT **Jean Louis Berlandier, a French botanist, sketched this Comanche family in west Texas in 1828. The huge buffalo robe also functioned as a rug for the tepee and as a bed for the family. (Berlandier. 1828)**

the burning heat of the summers and survive the numbing cold of the northern winds that blew during the bitter winters.

Although the Comanches developed a close relationship with their steeds, they were not sentimental about them. In the 1840s, when buffalo and deer were scarce, William Bollaert, an English traveler in Texas reported, "The Comanches had eaten twenty thousand mustangs in five years time."

From 1800 to 1865, the Comanches supplemented their store of tamed mustangs by stealing thousands of horses from Mexicans and Texans in what was the largest rustling operation in the history of the American West. Colonel Richard Irving Dodge complained, "For crawling into camp, cutting hobbles and lariat ropes, and getting off undiscovered with the animals they [the Comanches] are unsurpassed."

The horse, then, was the mainstay of the Comanche tribe. With them the Comanches were the lords of the Plains; without them they would have been reduced to not much more than foot-slogging scavengers.

Weapons

When the young Spotted Pony joined the ranks of warriors, the Comanches were equipped only with their traditional weapons: the club, lance, and bow and arrow. As the Comanches began to trade with the Comancheros, they acquired European weapons: knives, arrowheads, and lance points of steel, flintlock muskets, gunpowder, and lead bullets. Later, from unscrupulous Mexican and Texan traders, they acquired percussion cap rifles and pistols. After 1836 they came into possession of captured Colt revolvers, and in the twilight of their dominance in the mid-19th century they outgunned the US Cavalry with lever-action repeating rifles.

The mainstays of Comanche arms, however, were the traditional weapons used for both hunting and fighting. William Brown Parker, who took part in an expedition exploring frontier Texas in 1854, described a typical Comanche lance and shield.

Artist George Catlin wrote, "The usual mode of taking wild horses is by throwing the lasso while pursuing them at full speed. Dropping a noose over their necks soon checks them and they are choked down." During training, "Great care is taken, not to subdue the spirit of the animal." (Denver Public Library)

"The lance point was a straight piece of steel, about two feet and a half long and an inch wide [75 × 2.5cm], tapering to a point. This was fixed into a slender handle about four and a half feet [1.4m] long fashioned from a branch of the bois d'arc tree making the weapon seven feet [2m] in length." The handle, he described, was "ornamented with tufts of colored cotton yarn and strips of cloth worked with beads." Other lances could be as long as 14 feet (4.3m).

The Comanche shield, he described, was "round, and about two feet [0.6m] in diameter, made of wicker-work, covered first with deer skins and then with a tough piece of raw buffalo-hide drawn over it, making it proof against arrows. It was ornamented with a human scalp, a grizzly bear's claw and a mule's tail … fastenings for the arm were pieces of cotton cloth twisted into a rope."

Testimony to the toughness of the shields comes from Texan J. W. Wilbarger, whose brother was scalped during a Comanche raid. During that fight in 1844, he wrote: "Santa Anna, the Indian chief, suddenly dashed to the front, and holding his shield of buffalo hide before him, he ran along the line of his opponents. The whites all fired at him, but their balls only rattled harmlessly on his tough rawhide shield."

The major weapon of the Comanches was the bow and arrow discharged from horseback. Their bow was short, not more than 3 feet (1m) long, so it could be easily managed while riding a galloping horse. The Comanches made a bow from a branch of a bois d'arc or hickory tree. Sometimes they recurved the branch but usually they simply bent it into an arc. They made bowstrings from twisted buffalo or deer sinews.

Comanche arrows were carefully crafted to fly straight and true. They were constructed from straight branches of dogwood, ash, or mulberry trees. Comanche women boiled down horse or buffalo hooves to make a glue to attach turkey or buzzard feathers to the end of the shaft giving the arrow stability in flight.

Arrowheads were made of sharpened flint when the Comanche bands first ventured onto the Plains. Later, trading with the French, Spanish, and other Europeans, they procured steel or iron arrowheads. For hunting, they used a broad, thin, and flat arrowhead designed to be easily pulled from the quarry without tearing valuable meat. In contrast, arrowheads used in warfare were thick and barbed. To pull one out was to rip flesh and tear arteries, making a terrible and often fatal wound. If possible, the best method of extraction was to push the arrow through the body part, forcing it out on the opposite side of the entry wound. Combined with their superior horsemanship, the Comanches' skill with the bow made them the most deadly fighters on the Plains.

The Comanches' steel axes and butcher knives had great utilitarian value around the camp and in close-quarter fighting. Some Comanches preferred a smaller, thin-bladed knife for scalping, which was done in several deft moves, often from behind. The warrior first lifted up his downed enemy's hair. Pulling it back, he cut across the forehead at the hairline. Pulling on the hair, he worked his blade under the scalp and then peeled it off from the skull. The scalp was then ready to be attached to a lance, shield, or staff.

The Comanches' all-purpose knife had a heavy broad blade six to 12 inches (15–30cm) long, sharpened on one side only. It was suited more for butchering buffalo than for fighting. At close range, the Comanches preferred the tomahawk or a heavy war club.

The Comanches never learned the art of sophisticated knife fighting. They tended to hold the blade downward in a club-like grip in which they could only stab downward in an awkward manner. On the rare occasions when a Comanche warrior found himself in a knife fight with a Texan wielding a Bowie knife – held in a rapier grip, allowing stabbing and slashing in any direction – he usually came to an ugly end.

Firearms were adopted early in the 18th century. Flintlock muskets soon gave way to percussion cap weapons and finally to lever-action rifles with metallic self-contained cartridges. The Comanches were always short of ammunition and disciplined firing tactics were unknown to them.

Tactics

In their conflicts with other tribes for dominance of the Plains during the 18th century, a warrior gained prestige by reckless bravery. A Comanche would never surrender and though badly wounded would fight to the death.

The greatest valor was to be had by counting coup, in which a warrior struck (but did not kill) an enemy in hand-to-hand fighting. Scalping provided evidence of valor, and dried scalps were fixed to lances, horses, or tepees to display the warriors' prowess in battle.

Before launching a raid the warriors worked themselves into a fighting frenzy. Under a full moon they performed war dances in which the throbbing of drums, the roaring of battle songs, and the stomping, gyrating dance around a blazing fire created a fury of excitement and blood lust in the men.

Raids could cover hundreds of miles, so careful logistical preparations had to be made. The Comanches loaded their ponies with beans, sun-dried meat pounded into flakes, and pemmican, a concoction of meat fat, beans, and fruits. Each warrior took several horses on the raid. In case of pursuit it was necessary to switch from a tired mount to a fresh horse. If the retirement was leisurely, the extra horses could be loaded with plunder.

Before a raid the warriors turned their faces into hideous masks by painting them in lurid colors. They also painted their bodies and their horses in streaks of color and often with the magical signs of their individual putas (spiritual powers).

The usual purpose of a raid was to acquire loot, and stealing horses was always a primary objective. They preferred to steal by stealth alone, but if challenged, they would fight. When fighting against other tribes, Mexicans, or Spaniards, a payment of tribute might stay their usual brutalities. After acquiring their plunder, in case of pursuit, they usually split up into small parties to confuse their pursuers. When American settlers began to infringe on Comanche hunting grounds, the desire for plunder often gave way to a desire to kill the interlopers.

Comanche tactics were not too different from modern-day guerrilla warfare. Warriors struck swiftly and unexpectedly at an unprepared and numerically inferior foe. They preferred to ambush an enemy rather then to face him in head-on conflict, and they rarely made frontal attacks against a prepared foe. On rare occasions when they rushed a prepared enemy and took heavy casualties or if their war leader was killed, they quickly lost heart for the battle and withdrew.

They had no concept of holding ground and, in most situations, when attacked by equal or superior numbers they would quickly retreat and scatter. It was a different matter when their women and children were threatened. In that case, Comanche warriors would put up a stubborn defense until their families were able to escape.

In an attack against a circled wagon train, a small group of soldiers, or a stagecoach, they galloped in circles around their quarry, drawing closer at each circle while discharging volleys of arrows or bullets. When resistance slackened, they dashed at their foes and administered the

Texas pioneer John H. Jenkins described the Comanches: "The warriors were almost without exception large, fine-looking men [with] erect, graceful, well-knit frames and finely proportioned figures." Other observers said they were short, squat, and ugly. The kidnapping of many Mexican and Texan children adopted by the tribe and subsequent racial mixing may account for the different descriptions. (Berlandier, 1828)

coup de grace with lance, tomahawk, club, or knife. Before the advent of repeating arms they would wait for their opponents to fire and then rush them before they could reload.

In mounted attacks, a Comanche used a leather thong to support himself as he hung along the side of his horse opposite the enemy. From this position he leaned under the horse's neck to fire his rifle or discharge arrows.

The Comanches coordinated attacks by using bird or animal calls and sometimes by smoke signals. At night they found high places and lit signal fires. But during battle each warrior fought as an individual.

After a successful raid, the war party returned to its village driving stolen horses. The warriors then distributed their other loot to the elders and the women and children of the tribe. They paraded through the village waving bloody scalps and singing of their triumphs to the jubilation of the tribe.

If a raid went badly, and a war leader or many warriors were killed, the men slunk into camp with their faces blackened and the tails of their horses cut. The women wailed in lament and slashed their breasts with knives and cut off some of their fingers as an expression of their sorrow.

INTO BATTLE

In 1816, after successfully completing his vision quest (a search for spiritual power) and acquiring his puta, 16-year-old Spotted Pony was now a full-fledged warrior. To celebrate, his father presented him with a horse, and his older brother gave him a bow and a dozen arrows. From his mother, the young man received a buffalo hide shield with a picture of a spotted pony painted in red ocher in the center. Most prized of all was a 12 foot (3.7m) lance with a long Spanish-made steel spear point, a present from his uncle who had captured it in battle with a Cheyenne.

The young warrior was able to affix a buffalo tail to his lance, but he hungered for the tail of a stolen horse or an Apache or Spanish scalp to tie to his shield.

He and Buffalo Hump, his childhood playmate and elder by a year, embraced and vowed to bring honor to the Penatekas. They boasted that they would drive away the remaining Apaches, steal the Spaniards' horses and slaughter the Mexican settlers who attempted to penetrate their domain in central and southern Texas. There was glory to be had as the Spanish, weakened by defeats in Europe and racked by revolts in Mexico, loosened their already tenuous hold north of the Rio Grande.

Soon after the celebration, Spotted Pony and Buffalo Hump eagerly sat with the circle of elders. This was a special occasion, for the elders were planning a raid deep into Texas and northern Mexico. At that time the entire Penateka clan rarely met as one; however, some of its scattered bands attended the war council, perhaps because Spotted Pony's father had a reputation as a great warrior.

Spotted Pony and Buffalo Hump watched as a half dozen Kiowa warriors strode into the council meeting. For years the Comanches and Kiowas had been enemies contesting the right to hunt the buffalo herds roaming the Plains. When Spotted Pony was a young boy, the two tribes had made peace and agreed on a fighting alliance that was to last more than 70 years, during which time they fought side by side against all comers.

With flowing oratory the Kiowas announced that they had come to join with their brothers in a raid against the Spaniards. Then each of the elders, including Spotted Pony's father, rose and proudly recounted his record as a warrior. Spotted Pony's father was named the raid's leader after he told how he had slain buffalo with the lance, counted coup upon Apache warriors, stolen hundreds of horses, and taken the scalps of scores of Spaniards and Mexicans.

As he finished his oration he asked the warriors to join him in the raid. The more than 100 men present let out loud whoops and blood-curdling cries as all volunteered to join the war party into Mexico.

Spotted Pony was bursting with pride at his father's election, for Comanche war parties were made up of volunteers only. These fiercely independent warriors would follow only a man they respected and trusted and whose puta was strong and powerful.

That night, the men feasted on buffalo roasts and danced around a smoldering fire, chanting and boasting of their prowess in battle. They slept until shortly after dawn, then arose, ate, bade farewell to wives and children in their camp along the Clear Fork of the Brazos River, and silently rode south.

The war party crossed the Colorado River and rode into the high ground of the plateau country west of the Mexican settlement at San Antonio. They skirted San Antonio and continued south until they crossed the Rio Grande west of the small settlement at Laredo. This route into Mexico became known to Europeans as the Comanche Trace.

After crossing the river they watered their horses and rested. That evening they tested their bow strings and sharpened lance points and tomahawks with rough-edged rocks. A few of them checked the flints and gunpowder to be used with the rifles they had acquired in exchange for horses while trading with venturesome American merchants along the Red River.

The following morning, after munching a meal of sun-dried buffalo meat, they painted their faces with earthen colors of yellow, red, and black. Some painted their bodies and their horses with colored stripes and symbols of their puta. Then they mounted and rode toward the Mexican villages of Zaragoza, San Juan de Sabinas, Nueva Rosita, and their surrounding ranches.

The warriors rode with great confidence, knowing their prey were only lightly armed. The Spanish crown, plagued by sporadic revolutionary uprisings throughout New Spain, prohibited villagers from owning firearms. The only people permitted guns were soldiers, who were usually few in number and confined to the scattered presidio forts of the larger settlements. The raid, the Comanches knew, would consist more of slaughter than of warfare.

As the band approached a small ranch, the warriors launched a typical Comanche attack. Whooping and screaming battle cries, they galloped into the cluster of small houses. As the main force struck the homes of the hapless Mexicans, others rode into the corrals and cut out the horses.

Comanche warriors often practiced their mounted tactics. They would circle an enemy riding at full gallop while discharging a storm of arrows. As the enemy weakened they would charge home with their lances. (Catlin, 1836)

When the dozen or more ranchers, armed with nothing more than rakes, home-made swords, and an ancient blunderbuss, attempted to protect their families, they were struck down by a flurry of arrows. A coup de grace from a lance or a tomahawk finished the job.

Spotted Pony loosed an arrow at a Mexican aiming an old musket at Buffalo Hump. Struck in the chest, the Mexican fell to the ground, and Spotted Pony reined his horse to a stop and leaped from his saddle. Running to the fallen man, who was quivering with pain, Spotted Pony came up behind him, grabbed his hair and pulled back his head. Then slicing with his knife, he cut through the Mexican's forehead and filleted the scalp from his head.

Lifting the bloody trophy high, Spotted Pony let out a scream of triumph. Then he bent down and neatly slit the throat of the dying Mexican. Laughing in his blood lust, he ripped the pants from the dead man, cut off his privates and stuffed them in the Mexican's mouth.

Mounting his horse, he viewed the scene of carnage. He watched Buffalo Hump impale an aging woman with his lance and flip her into the air. As she fell to the ground, he leaned down from his mount and scalped her long gray hair.

Then Spotted Pony saw a plump teenage girl hiding behind a bale of hay. She whimpered in fear as he rode to her. The warrior leaped from his saddle, flung the hysterical girl to the ground, and raped her. He uncoiled his lariat and put the loop around her neck to keep her in check, then remounted and let out another scream of triumph. He, Spotted Pony, had killed and raped enemies of his people. His puta was powerful. He was a Comanche warrior. This was the way of the Penatekas.

When all of the men had been killed and a few of the more desirable women were spared to be taken as camp slaves, the Comanches set the ranch's buildings on fire and rode toward the villages. At each village, elders came out to meet the raiders waving white flags. Some held horses, while others offered clothes, blankets, or robes of cotton or wool sewn by the village women. Leather bridles and lariats were also proffered, while other elders offered a poor collection of iron pots, kettles, hatchets, or knives pounded out from scrap metal by the village blacksmith.

Offering the tribute, the elders begged that their women not be carried off, that their houses not be burned, and that they be left a few horses or mules in order to plow their fields. Haughtily the war chiefs accepted the tribute from two of the villages and left them in peace. The tributes of the third village, however, were too poor to accept, and the raping and killing repeated itself.

Finally sated, the band tied their loot onto the backs of captured horses. Leading and half dragging the captured women by the ropes around their necks, the Comanches turned north and marched toward the Rio Grande.

For days they kept up a leisurely pace without fear of pursuit. When some of the women, stumbling on foot, began to falter and drop from exhaustion, their captors allowed them to ride bareback on captured horses. The ropes were then transferred from the necks of the women to those of the horses. During the balmy evenings of late summer the women gathered firewood, did chores around the camp, and satisfied the warriors' physical needs.

When the warriors finally arrived at the Comanche camp at the Brazos River, they had completed a round trip of nearly 800 miles (1,300km). As they arrived, they were met by the women, children, and old men who, whooping and squealing with delight, banged drums and sang praises to the returning warriors.

Upon dismounting, the warriors proudly distributed the loot of the raid to their wives and mothers. The female captives were turned over to the Comanche women, who would force them to perform the more onerous duties around the camp and often abused or beat them. This was to be the unhappy lot of the captives until they were ransomed or died, or until they turned Comanche and were accepted as a member of the tribe. The children they bore during their captivity were considered to be full members of the tribe.

This raid was one of a pattern that swept the settlements in Texas and as far as the Mexican province of Durango, more than 200 miles (320km) south of the Rio Grande. Only the settlements in New Mexico were spared the ravages of Comanche raids, and this only because the Comanches enjoyed a lucrative trade with the merchants of Santa Fe and Taos. The Comanches offered horses, slaves, buffalo robes, and unwanted plunder in exchange for clothing and weapons.

During the next few years Spotted Pony learned the craft of the raider. He learned how to slip into a ranch or village and drive off the horses before sleepy ranch hands could react. He acquired a mental image of the waterholes, grazing grounds, passes through the hills, and locations best suited for ambushes. One day, after successfully stealing a brace of fine horses, he rode to the tent of an elderly brave and traded the mounts for the man's pretty daughter, who became his wife. He exhilarated in the wild, free, roving life of the Penatekas. He knew no master. He was one of the lords of the Plains.

By 1820, many of the Spanish frontier settlements were reduced to ashes. In the remainder, people lived in fear of the Comanche moon, a full moon during the late summer and fall when raids were most common. Most of the missions developed by the Catholic missionaries were deserted and in ruins. Villages were depopulated, and the frontier from Texas, Nuevo Leon, Coahuila, Chihuahua, and Tamaulipas was threatened with abandonment.

Armed with bow, arrows, and a 14 foot (4.3 m) lance, the mounted Comanches, considered the best riders and fighters, soon drove other competing tribes from the Southern Plains. They dominated Comancheria for 150 years. (*Pictorial History of Texas*)

THE COMING OF THE TEXANS

Just when all seemed lost for the Spanish, a frail man from the north named Moses Austin offered a solution. When Austin, an American, rode into San Antonio de Bexar during the fall of 1820 seeking permission from the Spanish overlords to settle 300 families on Texas lands, he was at first threatened with arrest. But cooler heads prevailed.

Austin and other empresarios convinced the Spanish authorities that the only way to prevent the destruction of the Spanish settlements in Texas and northern Mexico was to put a buffer of Norte Americano settlers between the Spanish and the rampaging Comanches. Let the well-armed gringos fight off the Indian raiders, they reasoned, while the Mexican colonies grew and prospered in peace. The argument made sense, and permission for the settlement was soon granted. This decision was to have momentous and unintended consequences – the influx of Americanos spelled doom for the Spaniards' Mexican successors and the Comanche bands.

The first 300 families were soon followed by others. First a trickle and then a flood of Americans poured onto the land. The newcomers, known as Texicans, initially settled in the eastern forest land and later moved into the riverine southern parts of Texas.

Spotted Pony and his fellow tribesmen at first skirted the Texan settlements and were indifferent to them. After all, those areas were not roamed by the main buffalo herds and they posed no problem to Comanche dominance of the Southern Plains. He and Buffalo Hump, now experienced warriors, continued raiding Mexico, avoiding the Texan settlements and thus outflanking what was supposed to be the protective buffer zone.

The strategic picture changed dramatically in 1821 when the Mexicans threw off the Spanish yoke, only to become embroiled in internal revolts. By 1836 the Texans had won their independence from Mexico, and the new country was flooded with hordes of new immigrants from the United States and Europe. As the white tide moved west, Spotted Pony and his fellow tribesmen viewed the newcomers with alarm.

The settlers were tall, lean, hard-eyed men. They came in wagons with their wives and children. They brought iron plows to dig up the land and long-barreled rifles that could kill a man at 200 yards (200m).

Unlike the Comanches, who considered the land to be a gift to the entire tribe, each Texan staked out a plot of land to call his own. Sometimes he built fences around it. He chopped down the trees to build a house, drove off or killed the game, planted crops, and threatened to kill anyone who trespassed or challenged his possession of the land.

The Texans not only seized the land, they also refused to pay tribute to the tribe. They were a people – many of Scots-Irish background – who were as rude, as tough, and as arrogant as the Penatekas. They regarded the Comanches as crude barbarians and sneered at their customs and beliefs. The Comanches soon determined in their tribal councils that these strange and dangerous people must be destroyed.

Attacking the Texans was an attractive proposition for other reasons too. Spotted Pony acknowledged that the interlopers possessed some beautiful large horses with which he could breed his mustangs. And their women had long blonde hair, which would look fine dangling from his shield.

The attack on Fort Parker

The first major clash between these two fierce peoples occurred in the early summer of 1836. The Parker clan, 38-strong, had settled a beautiful, uninhabited patch of land near the Navasota River in central Texas. Along with a few other frontier families, they had cleared the land, built cabins, and surrounded the settlement with a log stockade. During the day, most of the men worked in the nearby fields planting and maintaining their crops of corn.

On one bright day in May, Spotted Pony was riding with a war band of more than 100 braves, mostly Comanches accompanied by a few Kiowas. As they approached the Parker fort, one of the warriors tied a white flag to a pole.

There were only five men in the fort at that time: the clan elder, John Parker, his two sons, Benjamin and Silas, and Samuel Frost and his son. The rest were women and small children. Benjamin went out to parley with the Comanches, who told him they only wanted directions to a nearby stream and a cow to eat. When the young man refused to give them a cow, other Comanches rode up suddenly and killed Benjamin with lance thrusts. Letting out blood-curdling yells, they galloped into the fort.

The Comanches first obtained flintlock rifles from French traders who roamed across the plains in the 18th century. The French, who dominated the fur trade early in the century, eagerly traded guns, lead bullets, and gunpowder for buffalo hides. (Berlandier, 1828)

They rode down 79-year-old John Parker and speared him, scalped him and ripped off his genitals. His wife, "Granny" Parker, was pinned to the ground with a lance, her clothes torn off, and repeatedly raped. Silas Parker, Frost, and his son were killed trying to protect their women.

Lucy Parker, attempting to flee with her four children, was overtaken by the frenzied riders. They scooped up her young daughter, Cynthia Ann, and her six-year-old son, John, and carried them off. Two of the women in the fort were raped and wounded while Elizabeth Kellogg and Rachel Plummer were each raped and then dragged up onto a captor's horse, along with Rachel's infant son.

Pioneer and author James T. DeShields dramatically described the scene: "Murder, with bat-like wings brooded over the scene infernal, and drank in the Babel of piteous and fierce sounds."

As one warrior leaned from his horse to grab Lucy Parker, her pet dog leaped into the air and sunk its teeth into the horse's nose, "whereupon," DeShields reported, "horse and rider somersaulted into a gully." The warrior was the only Comanche casualty.

By this time the men working in the fields had grabbed their rifles and were running frantically to the fort. But it was too late. The Comanches rounded up all the horses in the Parker corral. They tied the two captured women to horses, took the three captured children up in their saddles and with cries of triumph rode out of the fort. They had killed five men, raped women, and stolen two women, three children, and a number of horses within only a few minutes. It was, Spotted Pony considered, a most successful raid.

The band pushed their ponies hard all day and into the evening. At midnight, according to Elizabeth Kellogg, they stopped and camped. Kellogg and the other prisoners were bound with rawhide and then thrown on their faces onto the ground. The Comanches and their Kiowa allies then erected a pole and built a large fire.

As the flames leaped into the midnight sky, the warriors, seemingly drunk with victory, held a scalp dance around the pole. Chanting and shouting, leaping into the air and waving bloody scalps, they re-enacted the murders they had committed during the day. The two women were stripped naked and were alternately beaten bloody with the warrior's bows and gang raped by the frenzied dancers.

The following morning the band divided the spoils. Elizabeth Kellogg was given to the Kiowas. Rachel Plummer and her child and the two Parker children were kept by the Comanches. Then the Kiowas rode out to the west while the Comanches headed to their northern settlements.

Elizabeth Kellogg was sold as a slave several times until she was eventually liberated when a band of Delaware Indians sold her back to some whites for $150 in ransom money. Rachel Plummer, escaped to a white settlement but soon died. Her son was later ransomed.

The Comanche bow was deadly within 60 yards (55m). Noah Smithwick, who fought Penateka warriors stated, "It gave them an advantage over the muzzle-loading rifle ... A Comanche could discharge a dozen arrows while a white man was loading a gun." (University of Texas Institute of Texan Cultures at San Antonio)

The Comanches held the two Parker children for years. John was finally ransomed, but Cynthia Ann was raised by the Comanches. She learned the language, was renamed Naduah, and became the wife of a warrior chief named Peta Nacona. In later years her son, Quanah Parker, became the last great war chief of the Quahadi Comanches, and led a band of 700 warriors in an attack on American buffalo hunters at Adobe Walls in 1874.

The massacre of the Parkers was the beginning of a murderous feud between the Comanche–Kiowa tribes and the Texans which was to last almost 40 years, with no quarter given or expected by either side.

The ferocity of the fighting can be judged by a description given by a warrior, Hunting Horse, of the death of a fallen Texas Ranger: "Lone Wolf got off his horse and chopped the man's head to pieces with his brass hatchet-pipe. Then he took out his butcher knife and cut open the man's bowels."

The Comanches realized these Texans were unlike the Mexican and Spanish settlers who had preceded them. They were well armed and well mounted and in a fight were just as ruthless as any Comanche. When the Comanches raided their settlements, posses of vengeful men called Rangers were quick to pursue and kill any tribesman who got in reach of their long rifles and their new six-shot revolver pistols.

LEFT **In 1835, the large Parker clan settled along the Brazos River and built a log stockade for protection against marauding Indians. On May 19, 1836, while most of the men were working in their cornfields a mile (1.6km) from the fort, a war party of Comanches burst into the stockade killing the few men inside and kidnapping a number of women and children. (***Border Wars of Texas***)**

BELOW **During the 1820s, when Americans poured into Texas, the Comanches singled out parties of surveyors for attack because they realized that when surveyors finished their work settlers would soon swarm onto the land. Surveying parties establishing boundaries of Spanish Land Grants or empresario boundaries usually consisted of no more than eight men. (Denver Public Library)**

When Texan farmers plowed new lands to the north and west, the full wrath of the Comanche bands fell upon them. Soon the Texas frontier, from the Rio Grande to the Red River, was the scene of killing, torture, and rape.

As the killing continued with increasing ferocity the Comanche chief Mukwarrah explained to Noah Smithwick: "The white man comes and cuts down the trees for houses. The buffalo are frightened and depart and the Indians are left to starve."

THE COUNCIL HOUSE FIGHT

In February 1840, a delegation of Comanches rode into San Antonio to tell Texan leaders they wished a treaty of peace with the whites. They were told that if they brought in every one of their white captives such a peace could be arranged.

On March 19, 32 warriors accompanied by 33 women and children rode into San Antonio bringing one prisoner, 15-year-old Matilda Lockhart. Twelve chiefs led by Mukwarrah and accompanied by Spotted Pony were escorted into the city's Council House while the rest of the Comanches camped around the building's grounds.

When the chiefs were seated, Colonel William S. Fisher, commanding the 1st Regiment of Texas Infantry, demanded to know where the rest of the white prisoners were being held. Mukwarrah replied that they were held by other bands.

But when the Texans questioned Matilda they heard another story. She told them that there were other white girls in the Comanche camp only a few miles from San Antonio. She said that the Comanches planned to ransom those prisoners one by one in order to get more loot from the Texans. Furthermore, the girl was in a pitiful state. According to James T. DeShields, "The girl's body was covered with bruises and

Daredevil riders, Comanches would circle a wagon train at the gallop while loosing a swarm of arrows and gunshots. If the defenders ran out of ammunition or suffered crippling casualties, the warriors would charge; if the Comanches overran the defenses, they would kill and mutilate the settlers. (Denver Public Library)

sores, her hair had been singed to the scalp and her nose had been burned off to the bone." Later the Texans found that most of her body had been seared with hot irons.

Upon hearing the girl's story, Colonel Fisher demanded that the Comanches bring in the remaining whites. Until then, he stated, the chiefs would be held prisoner in the San Antonio jail. As he spoke, Texas soldiers entered the Council House and surrounded the building.

When Mukwarrah shouted defiance, the Comanches pulled out the knives and tomahawks concealed in their robes; the Texans cocked their rifles or grasped their Bowie knives. Then the peace conference turned into a raging fight.

Spotted Pony, whose reflexes were still quick at 40 years of age, dashed for the door. As a soldier thrust at him with his bayonet, Spotted Pony slipped aside, stabbed the soldier in the side, then rushed through the door into the courtyard and onto the back of his pony. He galloped from the town.

Most of the Comanches were not so lucky. The fighting spilled out from the Council House into the street; the sound of gunshots mingled with screams of pain and rage. Fired at close range, the Comanches' arrows buried themselves up to the feathers in the breasts of their victims, while bullets smashed Comanche flesh and bone. Within moments Mukwarrah and his chiefs were sprawled dead on the floor of the Council House surrounded by the bodies of two Texas judges and a private soldier.

One Comanche dashed into a nearby stone building. When he refused to surrender, Texas soldier Hugh McLeod reported that, "A Mexican climbed onto the roof, tore a hole through the shingles and threw a flaming ball of rags soaked with turpentine onto the Comanche's head." Screaming, with his head and body in flames, he ran from the building and was "riddled with bullets."

By the time the fighting died down, seven Texans lay dead and eight were badly wounded. Thirty Comanche warriors died in the melee, along with three women and two children; 27 Comanche women and children and two old men were taken prisoner.

The following day an old Comanche woman was given a horse and sent to search for the Comanche camp. There, she told the warriors that the Texans had agreed to release their prisoners if the Comanches returned all

Expert horsemen, Comanches dodged enemy bullets by clinging to the side of their horses. Some learned to fire their rifles and sometimes discharge arrows from under their horse's neck. (Artist Unknown)

In August 1833, Josiah Wilbarger, journeying near Austin, was attacked by Comanches. Lying badly wounded, a warrior tore off his scalp. "It sounded," he said, "like an ominous roar and peal of distant thunder." Left for dead, he survived. (*Indian Depredations in Texas*)

their white prisoners unharmed. When the old woman related the news of the slaughter at the Council House, the wives, mothers, and daughters of the slain began to scream in horror. In Comanche fashion they slashed their arms, legs, and breasts while some cut off fingers.

Enraged, the Comanches turned on their captives. Thirteen women and children were stripped naked and tied to pegs driven into the ground. Then their bodies were sliced with knives, body parts were hacked off, some were skinned alive, and all were finally burned to death.

At the first outcries of grief, a woman captive named Webster, clutching her infant son, took advantage of the confusion and escaped from the camp. She left behind an older son named Booker. After the Comanches' orgy of slaughter only Booker Webster and a five-year-old girl were spared.

On April 3, Piava, a Comanche chief, rode into San Antonio offering a prisoner exchange. A few days later he returned with seven white captives, including Booker and the young girl. The Comanche prisoners were then moved from the jail to San Jose Mission where, after a time, they were allowed to wander away. Both sides accused the other of treachery, and from that time on the Comanches and the Texans were locked in a feud in which each side vowed to exterminate the other.

Thirsting for revenge after the Council House fight, Comanche bands gathered to plan the largest raid in the history of the tribe. Buffalo Hump, Spotted Pony's boyhood friend, was now the leading war chief of the Penatekas. Orating before the tribal council, he laid plans to sack two prosperous towns in south Texas. In early August 1840, a war party of more than 1,000 braves, led by Buffalo Hump and including Spotted Pony, headed south to the town of Victoria. On August 6, they swooped on the settlement, killing and plundering, and stealing as many as 3,000 horses and mules. Then they continued south to the Gulf Coast town of Linnville, which they sacked and burned.

On their slow retreat northward, burdened with loot, the Comanches were ambushed by Texans at Plum Creek and suffered heavy casualties. The Battle of Plum Creek forever broke the Comanche dominance in south Texas, and, while occasional minor raids continued, the tribe never again ventured south of San Antonio in large force. The rest of Texas, however, was not to be spared.

Other events occurred swiftly. While Sam Houston, the first President of Texas, favored a policy of conciliation with Indian tribes, his successor Mirabeau Buonaparte Lamar favored a policy of extermination. Lamar ordered a series of military campaigns against all Indian tribes in Texas using more than 1,000 soldiers and Texas Rangers. These forces drove out all the tribes from east Texas onto the plains and forced the Comanches into the country north of San Antonio. To raid south into Mexico, Spotted Pony and his fellow Penatekas now had to swing many miles to the west to avoid the ever-vigilant Rangers. For a short while, raids against Texas slackened.

Spotted Pony, now an elder of the tribe with two wives and two small sons, contented himself with hunting the buffalo and going on only an occasional raid into Mexico.

Friendly relations with the Germans

In 1846, the United States went to war with Mexico, causing the Comanches to avoid raiding into northern Mexico. Also during that time, thousands of German immigrants made the long trip across the Atlantic to Galveston. From there, they soon began to trek into the hill country of central Texas, long a Comanche stronghold.

The Germans' leader, Baron Ottfried Hans Von Meusebach, decided it was better to become friends with the Comanches and feed them rather than fight them. On January 22, 1847, Von Meusebach and a score of settlers, to the horror of many Texans, ventured into Comanche country. Upon arriving at a large Comanche camp, Von Meusebach laid down his rifle and walked disarmed into the warriors' midst.

Spotted Pony and other warriors were prepared to fight the outsiders, but the Baron's friendly manner soon mollified them. In a rare moment on the frontier, Germans and Comanches met in peace and good humor, and Meusebach and Texas frontiersman Robert Simpson Neighbors smoked the peace pipe with the tribe's elders.

Ferdinand Roemer, a German scientist, described the formidable Buffalo Hump during the meeting: "His body naked, a buffalo robe around his loins, brass rings on his arms, a string of beads around his neck … he had distinguished himself through great daring and bravery in expeditions against the Texas frontier."

Under a canopy of stars both parties mellowed in friendship. Seated around a blazing campfire the Germans began singing their folk and drinking songs; Buffalo Hump, Spotted Pony, Old Owl, Santa Anna, and other chiefs countered by chanting songs to their gods and dancing around the fire.

A treaty was soon reached whereby the Comanches permitted the Germans to establish settlements on the Llano River, almost 100 miles (160km) north of San Antonio. In return, the Comanches were to receive presents of food, clothes, and camp equipment every March at a meeting at the new town of Fredericksburg. To Spotted Pony's surprise, it was one of the few treaties rarely broken by either side.

Later in the year, however, this pleasant idyll was shattered when an epidemic of smallpox swept through the Comanche nation; a cholera epidemic followed. Men, women, and children suffered from burning fevers, broke out in ghastly pustules, and died miserable deaths. Warriors looked on impotently as Comanche folk medicines of incantations and sweat baths failed to defeat these invisible foes. Both of Spotted Pony's wives and his two children died in the epidemics.

In 1849 it was estimated that the Comanches numbered more than 20,000. Less than three years later, in 1851, their numbers had shrunk to fewer than 12,000. The Comanches never completely recovered from these depredations.

WAR ON THE FRONTIER

Resistance to the Comanche raids into Mexico was growing. In 1849, the Chihuahua legislature empowered "scalp hunters" to kill "troublesome Indians," particularly Comanches. The killers would be paid a handsome bounty for each scalp they brought to authorities in Chihuahua City. The legislation brought many gringo renegades into Mexico where they began to kill not only Comanches but any Indian who fell into their hands. The law was terminated, however, when John Joel Glanton, a former Texas Ranger, and his gang were accused of raiding isolated Mexican villages, killing and scalping the inhabitants and then claiming the bounty for Comanche scalps. Glanton's practice was, of course, much less dangerous and much more profitable than attacking Comanche warriors.

Following the end of the Mexican War in 1848, the US Army took jurisdiction over the Comanchero frontier and erected a chain of forts

New Mexico traders, called Comancheros, sold guns and steel implements to the Comanches in exchange for stolen horses, cattle, and captured Texans and Mexicans. Because of the trade, eastern New Mexico was usually spared Comanche raids. (Denver Public Library)

Cynthia Ann Parker was photographed after she was taken from a Comanche camp. Kidnapped, she once refused rescue, saying of her Comanche captor, "I love my husband ... and my little ones are his and I cannot forsake them." (Denver Public Library)

across central Texas from the Red River to the Rio Grande. At first the forts were garrisoned by 22 companies of the US Army; of these, 16 companies were infantry and, according to one Texas legislator "were as useful as lobsters" against Comanche raiders who could cover 50 miles (80km) in seven hours.

Then the army sent in two dragoon regiments to the frontier. Dragoons, who were little more than mounted infantry, were outfitted with unreliable single-shot pistols, muskets with limited range that could not be fired accurately from horseback, and heavy cavalry sabers. A dragoon wielding a saber stood little chance against Comanche warriors like Spotted Pony armed with long lances.

The Texas Rangers, feared by the Comanches because of their six-shot Colt revolver pistols, unkindly remarked that the greatest danger the Comanches faced from the dragoons was that seeing them in action would cause the warriors to laugh themselves to death. The dragoons, however, were soon replaced by lighter, faster, more flexible and better armed cavalry units.

During the late 1840s and early 1850s fraternization was not unknown between Comanche warriors and American soldiers. At Fort Chadborne in central Texas in 1852, Buffalo Hump and Spotted Pony attended games and horse races between soldiers and warriors. Colonel Richard Irving Dodge reported that horse races over short distances were almost always won by the fleet Comanche ponies, which outran the heavier cavalry mounts. The Comanches, who were inveterate gamblers, won a large number of saddle blankets, money, and leather goods from the cavalrymen.

The camaraderie, however, was not permanent. The good times were frequently interrupted when the Comanches gave up peaceful pursuits and raided outlying homes on the frontier.

One white man tried to bring peace to the troubled Texas frontier. When gold was discovered in California in 1849, Robert Neighbors persuaded Buffalo Hump to guide him in surveying a trail from central Texas to the New Mexico border. With 100 warriors, including his old friend Spotted Pony, Buffalo Hump escorted Neighbors and two surveyors to the border where the Rio Grande turns north at El Paso del Norte, and then returned to their camp in central Texas.

Neighbors was one of the few Texans who both understood the Comanches and cared about their welfare. In his peace-making efforts he had a temporary ally in Buffalo Hump. At tribal councils, Buffalo Hump counseled peace to his fellow chiefs. He pointed out that in 1840 when the Comanches were numerous and strong they had failed to destroy the Texans; now when they were weak they must make peace or be destroyed themselves.

The flaw in his reasoning lay in the increasing demise of the buffalo herds as Texans continued to extend their settlements further and further west and north. As the frontier advanced, the buffalo herds, reduced in size by white hunters, continued to migrate north with the consequence that hunting for the southern Comanches became less and less productive. By 1852 many of the Penatekas were starving. Ketumae, a Penateka warrior, in a roughly translated, plaintive appeal to Indian Agent Horace Capron, stated: "The game, our main dependence is killed and driven off and we are forced to starve. We see nothing but extermination. Give us some land we can call our own and where we may bury our people."

Nothing, however, was done to alleviate their suffering until September 24, 1853, when Neighbors was appointed Indian Agent for Texas. Neighbors met with the chiefs who agreed to settle on a reservation if Texas would provide them with food and clothing and keep whites from moving onto their land.

Although there was strong opposition by many Texans, the legislature provided 18,000 acres (7,000ha) near the Brazos River. By the summer of 1856 more than 800 Penatekas, including Buffalo Hump and Spotted Pony, had settled on the reservation. Other Comanche bands and the remainder of the 1,200 Penatekas moved north to unoccupied land and continued raiding.

The peaceful interlude on the reservation lands was short lived. Texans complained that the Penatekas used the reservation as a base from which they continued to raid frontier farms and ranches. The Comanches complained that Texans continued to kill their buffalo and encroach on their lands. Both complaints were probably correct.

On the Comanche side, perhaps men like Buffalo Hump and Spotted Pony were simply too old to change their ways. In August 1856 Buffalo Hump, Spotted Pony, and several dozen young firebrands struck settlements near Bandera in the Texas hill country and made off with dozens of mules. After selling them to a band of Choctaws, they returned to the reservation and made an appearance of meekness as they drew rations of coffee, sugar, and corn. The charade fooled no one, however, and they soon left the reservation to continue their nomadic ways. By the winter of 1856–57 only 400 Penatekas, mostly women and children, remained on the reservation.

The raids to the west and north of San Antonio continued even though more than one-fourth of the US Army was now stationed in Texas. Early in 1858, the Texas legislature commissioned the famous Indian fighter Captain John Salmon "Rip" Ford of the Texas Rangers to attack and destroy hostile Comanches wherever he found them. Early in May, Ford crossed the Red River into Oklahoma, where he had no jurisdiction, with 100 Rangers and more than 100

Matilda Lockhart was gathering pecans during the winter of 1838 when Comanches kidnapped her. To prevent her escape they burned the soles of her feet. She was ransomed reasonably quickly but soon died. (*Indian Depredations in Texas*)

Tonkawas, blood enemies of the Comanches. On May 11, Ford's scouts located a Comanche camp in the Washita valley.

At dawn the next morning they attacked. The Comanche warriors, 300 strong led by Iron Jacket, put up a fierce resistance that raged for more than seven hours. The rapid fire of the Rangers' six-shot revolvers was the determining factor in the battle. Eventually, Iron Jacket and his surviving warriors fled, leaving behind 76 dead. Ford lost two Rangers killed and two wounded; Tonkawa casualties are unknown.

In September 1858 army units and Texas Rangers launched a joint punitive expedition against the Comanches. On October 1, US Cavalry units aided by a band of Tonkawa tribesmen struck Buffalo Hump's camp in the Wichita Mountains in north Texas near the Oklahoma border.

On May 27, 1839, Captain John Bird and 31 Rangers were attacked by 300 Comanches. Bird and six others were killed. As the warriors prepared to finish them off, a young German, James Robinett, shot and killed their chief. Grief-stricken, the Comanches withdrew. (*Border Wars of Texas*)

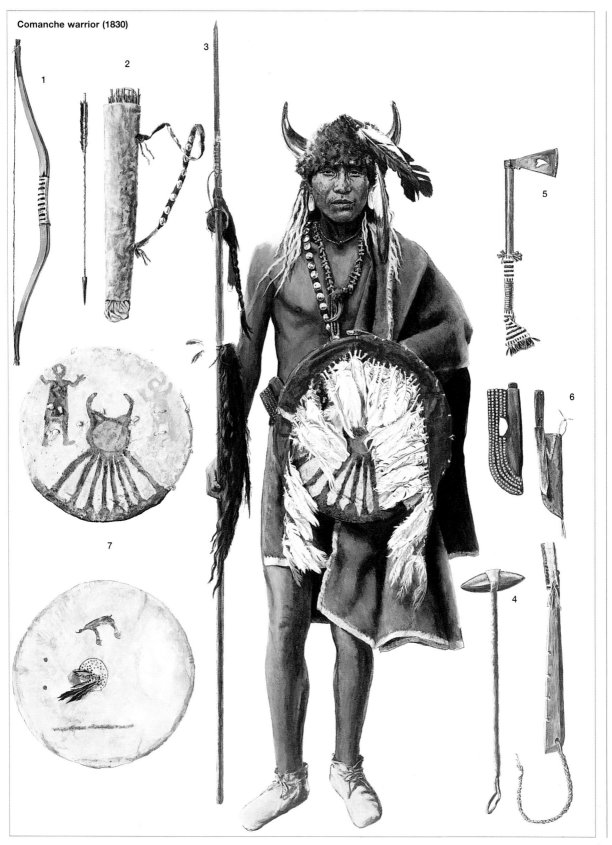

Comanche warrior (1830)

Camp life

B

The buffalo hunt

Trading with the Comancheros

E

Attack on the wagons

F

The battle of Plum Creek

G

H

Attacking shortly before dawn while most of the 500 Penateka men, women, and children were asleep, the troopers and their Indian allies galloped into the camp shooting into the tepees. Spotted Pony picked up his bow while others grabbed their rifles and stumbled out into the dim morning light and a sea of confusion. As the Comanches tried to put together an organized line of resistance, the cavalrymen kept up a continual fire on the camp while the Tonkawas stampeded the Comanche horses.

The surprised Penatekas rallied to Buffalo Hump while Spotted Pony and others sent volleys of arrows into the attackers and retreated into a ravine at the foot of the camp. Crouching behind sheltering rocks, Spotted Pony looked in horror as the cavalrymen shot down men, women, and children fleeing from their tepees. Even worse, the Tonkawas scalped the fallen bodies and then tauntingly waved their bloody trophies over their heads.

From the protection of the ravine, the Comanche warriors loosed a volley of arrows and bullets that caused their attackers to fall back to the village. There, the attackers set fire to tepees and food supplies. As the camp went up in flames, the cavalrymen and the Tonkawas, herding the Comanche horses before them, rode off to the south.

When the smoke cleared the survivors crept out of the ravine. They counted 56 of their brethren, men, women, and children, dead in the smoldering remains of their camp. The Comanches had killed five soldiers and wounded 12.

Mrs Rachel Plummer was pregnant when captured at Fort Parker. Six months later she gave birth to a baby boy. "A warrior tore him from my arms ... tied a rope around his neck, mounted his horse and galloped until my innocent was torn to pieces." (*Indian Depredations in Texas*)

The Comanches are expelled from Texas

With whites and Comanches continuing to indiscriminately murder each other, in June 1859, the Texas legislature acted. The government ordered the Texas reservations to be abandoned and the Indians to be moved onto new reservations in the Oklahoma Territory.

On September 1, Robert Neighbors wrote his wife, "I have this day crossed all the Indians out of the heathen land of Texas." Returning to Texas, where his stewardship of the Comanches had made him many enemies, he was shot in the back and killed by a white man on September 4. The Comanches had lost their last friend in Texas.

The result, according to Texas historian J. Frank Dobie, was that "No Indian had any business in Texas. If he came now, it was at his own peril, and it was the duty of any Texan to kill him and then inquire into his intentions. The Indians, however, continued to come in spite of the danger."

Buffalo Hump, Spotted Pony, and the remnant of their band settled briefly on the Oklahoma reservation north of the Red River. But the aging friends could not be contained for long and they soon led a raid into the Mexican province of Coahuila, bringing back much plunder to sell on the reservation. The raid covered a distance of more than 1,100 miles (1,800km) on horseback, quite a feat for two war chiefs in the sixth decade of their lives.

But overall, their situation was becoming desperate. The Comanches had a price on their heads in Mexico; Texas Rangers held open season on them; and the US Army was beginning to monitor their movements. Things were looking grim for those Comanches who refused to give up their wild life of raiding and mayhem. Suddenly, however, they received a welcome reprieve.

Both sides charged treachery when a "peace conference" degenerated into a pitched battle between Texans and Comanches in San Antonio's Council House in 1840. The Comanches plotted revenge and in the summer of that year they raided Victoria and burned Linnville to the ground. (*Border Wars of Texas*)

An open clearing surrounded by brush and forest called Comanche Flats was the scene of the ambush of the Linnville raiders by outraged Texans. Called the Battle of Plum Creek, the fight broke the power of the Comanches in south Texas. (Photo by Donald Brice, Texas State Library)

In November 1860 when a splintered nation elected Abraham Lincoln President of the United States, the simmering question of slavery boiled over and the southern slave states began to secede from the Union. On February 23, 1861, the people of Texas voted approval of a state convention's ordinance of secession from the federal government. The failure of United States troops to stop Comanche raids on the frontier was cited as one of several reasons that the western and northern counties voted to leave the Union.

On March 2, 1861, since Texas no longer owed allegiance to the United States, federal troops numbering almost 3,000 marched out of the frontier forts; they would later fight against their former Texan countrymen. Texans now faced two sets of implacable foes: the US Army and Navy on the one hand, and the Comanche and Kiowa tribes on the other. Worse, almost all Texan men aged between 18 and 50 were needed to fight in the Civil War, leaving the frontier dangerously exposed.

During the early days of confusion, caused by the war that pitted white against white, the Oklahoma reservation was seized by soldiers of the Confederate States of America. But they were soon called to other duties and in October 1862, Indians allied with the Union attacked the reservation, burning the buildings and scattering the Penatekas and other tribes who had sought refuge there. While Buffalo Hump drifted away into obscurity, Spotted Pony and other warriors saw an opportunity to revenge themselves along the virtually unprotected Texas frontier.

But first, the Tonkawas, who now lacked Union support, were dealt with. Considered traitors because of their alliance with the US Cavalry, the Comanches and Kiowas slaughtered most of the Tonkawa tribesmen. Fueling the Comanches' anger was their belief that the Tonkawas had once feasted on the flesh of one of their chiefs.

Both Union and Confederate emissaries courted the Plains Indians, offering them presents and treaties to either fight their enemies or simply to refrain from raiding their lines of communications. Soon, however, the warriors realized the vulnerability of the white frontier settlements, from southern Kansas to northern Mexico. Although afflicted with arthritis and blurring eyesight, Spotted Pony was rejuvenated by the thought of a Texas frontier protected only by volunteer militia composed mostly of older men and young boys. Now, he swore, while the whites were weak, he and his fellow Penateka warriors would strike and drive them back from the Plains.

Soon, the frontier was littered with burning homes, looted corrals, and the butchered bodies of Texan men, women, and children. Hundreds of whites were slain in the renewed Comanche fury. In whirlwind sorties, the warriors attacked wagon trains, stagecoaches, and mail riders. Stripping the drivers and tying them to the wheels of their overturned vehicles, the Comanches first slashed their captives' bodies and then burned them alive.

Isolated from the larger towns, with supplies not available, mail not delivered, and commerce destroyed, the Texas frontier receded more than 100 miles (160km) to the south and east. Abandoned and burnt houses marked the line of white retreat.

The US government steps in

The federal government, meanwhile, became fearful that the Santa Fe Trail would be cut by the rampaging warriors. The trail, stretching from St. Louis, Missouri, to Santa Fe, New Mexico, was the Union's main line of communications to the west.

In April 1863, Spotted Pony and other Comanche and Kiowa chiefs, garbed in full-feathered headdresses, buffalo robes, and deerskin clothes journeyed to Washington, D.C., as guests of the United States government. Riding part of the way on the railroad train they called the "iron horse," for the first time they realized the size, scope, and high population of the white man's domain.

After lengthy discussions the chiefs signed a treaty in which they promised not to raid along the Santa Fe Trail. They also agreed to return all white captives. Nothing, of course, was said about ceasing raids against the Texans.

In return, the US government agreed to set aside $25,000 annually for the Indians to be used for food, clothing, and shelter. Both sides agreed to the terms and in a mood of harmony the chiefs boarded the train to take them back to Missouri. From there they rode back to Comancheria to spread the good news and await their presents.

Unknown to the tribes, however, the United States Senate had refused to confirm the treaty; to the American Indian Commissioners the agreement became a dead issue. Not so to the expectant Indian tribes who believed they had made a solemn treaty with the white man.

Placido, chief of the Tonkawas, scouted for the Texas Rangers when they were pursuing Comanche raiders. The two tribes hated and fought each other. On occasion Tonkawas were known to eat captured Comanches. (*Pictorial History of Texas*)

During the late fall months of 1863, with winter approaching, Comanches and Kiowas gathered along the Arkansas River in Oklahoma and Kansas to wait for their largesse. Other tribes, including Cheyennes and Dakotas, also gathered to receive the promised gifts.

When they finally learned they were to receive nothing from the "white eyes," the Indians flew into a collective rage. Spotted Pony, who still believed that the Council House incident had been a calculated white man's trap, again felt betrayed. Furious, he and his fellow tribesmen took to the war path with a renewed sense of vengeance.

But there were compelling reasons for the Comanches to co-operate with the federal government. Union agents in New Mexico and Oklahoma, searching for a supply of beef for the hundreds of thousands of Union soldiers in the eastern, northern, and western states, eyed the

On the orders of Texan President Lamar, John H. Moore, leading 90 citizen-volunteers, surprised a Comanche village on October 24, 1840. Swooping down on them during a rainstorm, they slaughtered 130 men, women, and children. (*Border Wars of Texas*)

vast cattle herds of the rebel Texans' ranches. The agents approached the plains warriors and offered generous prices for every head of beef the Comanches could deliver to New Mexico and Oklahoma cattle dealers. Soon the Comanches, once North America's premiere horse thieves, became the continent's most accomplished cattle rustlers.

The Texan ranchers abandoned their horses and herds, and Spotted Pony and his cronies, who were used to running off stolen horses at the gallop, had to learn how to herd the plodding longhorn cattle. The longhorns could be easily spooked by a gunshot, roll of thunder, or lightning bolt, turning them into a mob of crazed beasts that ran frantically in every direction. In such situations it took hours, even days, to round up the cattle and head them to market.

Howitzers at Adobe Walls

In 1864, after an absence of almost a quarter of a century, Spotted Pony and the Penatekas again appeared in full force to raid ranches near San Antonio and the hill country north of Austin. The Penatekas had invested in modern rifles, six-shooter pistols, and ammunition instead of spending all their cattle money on clothing, trinkets, steel arrowheads, lance points, knives, and kettles. They were now armed as well as, and sometimes better than, their white enemies. When protests by Union officers had attempted to end the trade of cattle for guns, Comanchero traders ventured out onto the plains to secretly rendezvous with the warriors.

At the same time that they were taking the Union's money for beef, the Penatekas and Kiowas made an alliance with the Cheyennes and other

Northern Plains tribes to raid Union stagecoach stations and supply trains along the Santa Fe trail. They also attacked wagon trains carrying emigrant families to California, torturing and butchering the hapless people, who had headed west to escape the horrors of the Civil War.

In November 1864 the government ordered the famed western scout, Colonel Christopher "Kit" Carson, to crush the raiders and secure the Union's communication and supply lines. Leading a regiment of 350 New Mexicans, accompanied by 75 Ute and Apache scouts, and equipped with two mountain howitzers and more than a score of supply wagons, Carson led a march into the Panhandle country of north Texas.

On November 25, Carson's scouts located a Kiowa village near the ruins of an old trading post called Adobe Walls. Large numbers of Kiowas and Comanches had made winter quarters along the South Canadian River near the eroded walls of the old fort that had once protected the trading post. An estimated 3,000 Indians had camped in the area, for there was good water and fine grazing land along the river. There were also buffalo herds in the vicinity and the hunting was good.

On the morning of November 26, Carson's men attacked the Kiowas, taking them by surprise and causing Kiowa men, women, and children to flee in disorder to a large Comanche camp nearby. After scattering the Kiowas, Carson regrouped his troops around the ruins of Adobe Walls.

The Comanches, meanwhile, hearing the gunfire, reached for their rifles, mounted their horses and gathered up the Kiowa warriors into a large war party. Pausing briefly, they put on their war paint and chanted their war songs. Then, more than 1,000 strong, they spurred their mounts into a charge on the Union forces.

The howitzers opened up. The unearthly scream of shells was followed by devastating blasts amid the warriors' ranks. Startled, the warriors wheeled their horses, and rode back out of range. But screaming exhortations from Spotted Pony and other chiefs caused them to rally and charge back through the shell bursts.

The Comanches and Kiowas circled the soldiers' camp at full gallop, inflicting casualties by firing their rifles while hanging under their horses' bellies. Carson's men were holding their own, but their leader feared the warriors would discover his supply wagons, which were still slogging along several miles west of the fighting. The wagons would be easy targets for Comanche attackers.

Carson signaled his bugler to call for a fighting retreat. The troopers mounted as the howitzers fired away, and returned fire from horseback while the howitzers were hitched up to teams of horses. Then the entire force pulled out of Adobe Walls at the gallop.

In 1842, during a rainstorm, Texas Ranger Shapley Ross clashed with Comanche Chief Big Foot. Their pistols misfired and both drew knives. Lunging, Big Foot slipped and Ross skewered him. (*Indian Depredations in Texas*)

Meeting his supply wagons a short time later, Carson steered his force back to New Mexico.

Later Carson claimed a great victory. True, his forces had suffered far fewer casualties than had the Comanches. But according to Comanchero traders, caught in the Comanche camp during the battle, only the two howitzers had saved Carson's force from being annihilated. Carson never again ventured into Comancheria.

Both the Northern and Southern Plains Indians considered themselves at war with the United States. By the spring of 1865 both the Santa Fe Trail and the strategic Overland Trail which stretched from St. Louis, Missouri, to El Paso, Texas, through Tucson, Arizona, and on to Los Angeles and San Francisco, California, were virtually closed to commercial traffic.

Ineffective treaties

In April, after Confederate General Robert E. Lee surrendered to Union General U. S. Grant, the Confederacy ceased to exist. But as peace returned to the eastern and southern states, the war on the plains grew in intensity.

In October, US Indian Commissioners again met with the plains tribes in an effort to make peace. Spotted Pony and other tribal chiefs again smoked the peace pipe and listened, albeit with considerable skepticism, to what the Commissioners had to say. In what was to be called the Little Arkansas Treaty, the government offered the Comanches and Kiowas free rein in western Oklahoma and the Texas Panhandle. The government also would provide each Indian with $15 in cash or produce annually for a period of 40 years.

Since there were large buffalo herds roaming free in the allotted areas, Spotted Pony and others believed the funds would enable them to buy new rifles, ammunition, and good blankets. But when the government supplies arrived they consisted of moldy Civil War army rations and cheap blankets that fell apart in rain or snow.

As with other treaties between Indians and whites, both sides soon violated the letter and spirit of the agreements. Warfare on the plains continued.

The federal government gave command of the area that included Comancheria to Lieutenant-General William Tecumseh Sherman, famous

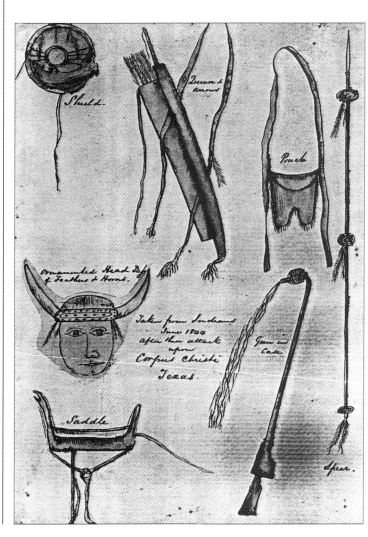

William Bollaert, an adventurous Englishman who spent two years roaming the Texas frontier, sketched these weapons and other Comanche equipment which were captured from a war party that raided the coastal city of Corpus Christi in 1844. (*William Bollaert's Texas*)

for devastating the southern states during the Civil War. He was said to have stated, "The only good Indian is a dead Indian," and his policies seemed to mirror that thought. He banned payment of ransom to the Comanches for the return of white prisoners, maintaining that it only encouraged them to kidnap settlers. The Comanches responded by simply killing all their prisoners.

Again the federal government tried for another treaty, and at Medicine Lodge Creek in southern Kansas in October 1867, the chiefs received a wagon train loaded with gifts for them. The tribesmen agreed to give up Comancheria in exchange for three million acres (1.2 million ha) of reservation land in southwestern Oklahoma. They signed the treaty, probably tongue-in-cheek, and agreed to stay within the boundaries of the new reservation. The government also promised to provide schools for their children and to send instructors to teach the Comanches how to become farmers.

Ten Bears, a warrior of the Yamparika Comanches had this to say of the treaty: "My people have never first drawn a bow or fired a gun against the whites ... Following the buffalo, that my wives and children might have their cheeks plump and their bodies warm ... the soldiers fired upon us ... The blue-dressed soldiers came from out of the night ... and instead of hunting game they killed my braves ...

"The Comanches are not weak and blind. We took the war road ... and the white women cried and our women laughed ... there were no enclosures and everything drew a free breath ...

"Now the Texans have taken away the places where the grass grew ... If the Texans had kept out of my country, there might have been peace ... but my young men have danced the war dance."

THE SLAUGHTER OF THE BUFFALO

Spotted Pony and his fellow warriors accepted the goods and, after the Commissioners left, probably had a good laugh. Perhaps it was Spotted Pony who voiced the contempt for the white man's treaty. To the Penatekas, the ability to ride free was life itself. They gloried that their very name sent chills down the spines of the white eyes and other Indian tribes. It was they who drove out the Spanish and slaughtered the Mexicans. It was the Penatekas who fought the evil Texas Rangers to a standstill, and it was they who considered every horse in the West rightfully to belong to them. To think that the lords of the plains would spend their lives learning to walk behind a mule and plant vegetables!

Spotted Pony eased his aching bones on a buffalo robe and sat by the council fire smoking his pipe and fingering his new lever-action repeating rifle. This now fabled warrior spoke to the young warriors gathered around him, saying that as long as the buffalo roamed the plains and there were horses to steal, the Penateka would remain the lords of the plains. Sadly, for both whites and Comanches, he was terribly wrong.

In Texas, meanwhile, things had gone from bad to worse. Although the US Army had reoccupied its forts in the north near the Santa Fe Trail, the Texas frontier was still virtually unprotected. The Reconstruction government of Texas, backed by Union forces, had abolished the Texas

When Texas entered the American Union in 1846, the United States Army constructed a chain of forts along the frontier settlements from the Red River to the Rio Grande. They provided a haven for pioneer families but were unable to prevent constant raids on the scattered farms and ranches on the frontier. (*Pictorial History of Texas*)

Rangers and other state troops. Moreover, Union troops in Texas were stationed in the eastern and southern cities to support the newly imposed government. Along the frontier the carnage continued.

During the winter, Comanche warriors huddled in the Oklahoma reservation and accepted government food supplies. But in the spring, when their ponies shed their winter coats and the grass began to sprout up over the Plains, they began to plan new raids into Texas and Mexico. If in gentler societies the coming of spring turned a young man's fancy to courtship, for the young Comanche warriors it was a time for stealing horses and killing whites.

The raiders managed to put General Sherman into a rage when old Spotted Pony and a band of young followers raided Fort Dodge in Kansas and ran off with the army's herd of horses. During the winter of 1869, Sherman launched an attack against the Comanches and other plains warriors in Oklahoma and also in the Llano Estacado, or Staked Plains. The Llano Estacado, in northwest Texas and northeastern New Mexico, is a giant mesa, or plateau, of open grassy plains thrust upward by geological forces; a treeless grassland, with few waterholes. There are three deep canyons which stretch finger-like into the plateau, including Palo Duro Canyon which was to be the scene of the final campaign against the Comanches.

Sherman's offensive forced many of the free-ranging Comanches back onto reservation land, but the general nearly lost his scalp in the process. In May 1871, Spotted Pony and a band of Penatekas and Kiowas raided near the flourishing north Texas town of Jacksboro. At that time General Sherman was conducting an inspection of western outposts accompanied by only a small escort of troopers. One of the band's young scouts spied the small party and quickly reported the potential prey. Just as the band was about to descend on the general, another scout reported sighting a supply train a few miles out of Jacksboro. Deciding that loot was more important than killing a few soldiers, Spotted Pony and his friends attacked and subsequently looted the supply wagons. Scalp intact, General Sherman made it safely to Fort Sill, Oklahoma.

In that same year, a new and commanding war chief became the leader of much of the Comanche resistance. Quanah Parker was the son of the Comanche war chief Peta Nocona and the kidnapped Cynthia Ann Parker. Born in the late 1840s or early 1850s, he learned the way of the Comanches while growing up in the camp of the Quahadi clan. He grew into a muscular 6 feet (1.8m) in height, towering over his brother warriors. With a keen mind and strong body, and a talent for raiding and fighting, by the time he was in his twenties he had emerged as a tough, clever war leader.

Refusing to recognize any treaty with the white man, he led a band from his lairs in the Llano Estacado and raised havoc among the farmers and ranchers attempting to settle in north Texas and the Panhandle. In October 1871, Quanah sent Colonel Ranald Mackenzie, the army's best Indian fighter, into a towering rage when he slipped into the colonel's camp and stole 70 of his best horses.

At this crucial point, the very culture and existence of the Comanches came under threat from an unexpected quarter. After the Civil War, the eastern states experienced a fashion craze for buffalo robes. The demand for hides sent prices rising, and thousands of eager hunters traveled to the plains to hunt the huge beasts. The hides collected by the hunters were transported quickly and economically to the eastern markets by the new railroad line to Kansas. Buffalo numbers dropped astonishingly fast. While in 1865 it was estimated that more than 15 million buffalo roamed the Plains, a decade later buffalo were counted only in the thousands, and these survivors continued to be hunted without mercy.

To get revenge on the Comanches who had driven them from the plains, Lipan Apaches often scouted for the Rangers. In 1845, Flaco, an Apache chief, and Ranger Captain Jack Hays charged a Comanche war band and scattered them while armed only with revolver pistols. (*Indian Depredations in Texas*)

Indian complaints to the government about the slaughter on their reservation lands fell on deaf ears. Worse, rumors spread that some army posts were issuing free ammunition to the hunters. The Indians realized they were facing genocide. How could Comanche hunters feed their families now that the plains had become a desert littered with bleached buffalo bones?

Outraged, the famed Comanche warrior Kicking Bird said: "The buffalo is our money, the only resource with which to get what we need. We love the buffalo as the white man loves his money. They are killing the buffalo given to us by our Great Father in the Sky to furnish us with meat to eat and means to get things to wear."

The second Battle of Adobe Walls

In desperation, Quanah Parker, Spotted Pony, and other Comanche chiefs met with Cheyenne war chief Stone Calf and a large band of his warriors. They determined that they must destroy the buffalo hunters or their way of life would perish and their families would starve.

At the meeting, a Comanche prophet, Isa-tai or Rear-End-of-a-Wolf, orated that he had mystical powers and that his puta would make the white man's bullets unable to penetrate the warriors' skin. Isa-tai then organized a great dance in which the rot-gut whiskey provided by Comancheros played a key part.

In June 1874, a fired-up war party of 700 angry Indians prepared to attack 23 buffalo hunters camping near the ruined fort at Adobe Walls.

The hunters, along with a few merchants, had built several houses out of logs or sod a mile (1.6km) east of the ruins. The saloon, blacksmith shop, storehouse, and restaurant were portents of what could happen if more white settlers were allowed to farm and ranch on the Plains. As such, the war party was determined to destroy them.

After a night of full moon, on the pale dawn of June 27, the combined war party of Comanches, Kiowas, and Cheyennes, secure in the knowledge they were protected by Isa-tai's great puta, launched a mounted frontal attack. Faces daubed with red and yellow war paint, scalps flying from their lances and the bridles of their mustangs, and screeching their terrifying war cries, the warriors thundered down on the camp. Circling the ramshackle wooden buildings, they clung to the far side of their mounts, firing rifles or loosing arrows from beneath the throats of their horses.

Among the hunters, two brothers, Ike and Shorty Shadler, asleep in their wagon as the attack began, were quickly shot and scalped. The rest of the hunters took refuge in three buildings, firing at the circling horsemen from windows and chinks in the log walls. Riding at full gallop the Comanches and their allies were difficult targets, but the hunters' heavy .50 caliber Sharps buffalo rifles began to take a toll on the attackers.

At one point in the battle, a Comanche warrior was shot down near the door of one of the buildings. Quanah, leaning over his saddle, braved the hunters' fire, and rode to his fallen comrade. He scooped him from the ground, flung him over his pony's back and rode off unscathed.

Uniquely, the warriors put some army tactics into practice. Warriors attacked, circled the buildings shooting, and then at a bugle call, fell back and regrouped. When the bugler blew the charge, they attacked again. Years later, Quanah would recount that the bugler was an army deserter who had joined the tribe. Wearing war paint and a feathered bonnet, he blew army bugle calls to direct the fighting.

The battle slackened at noon when Quanah's horse was shot dead, spilling the chief onto the ground where he was struck in the shoulder by a spent bullet. The war party then conducted a desultory siege for four days before withdrawing in frustration. They had killed only four whites but had suffered 15 killed and 75 wounded from the lethal fire of the buffalo guns. They had learned the hard way not to launch frontal attacks against experienced hunters armed with guns with telescopic sights.

At Medicine Lodge Creek, Kansas, in October 1867, Comanches and allied tribes met American Commissioners. Refusing reservation life, Ten Bears, a warrior of the Yamparika Comanches said, "I was born on the prairie where the wind blows free ... The whites took the country we love. We wish only to wander on the prairie until we die." (Denver Public Library)

The surviving warriors considered torturing Isa-tai but finally decided against it. They declared his name, Rear-End-of-a-Wolf, to be an apt description of his puta and left him to ridicule.

The second Battle of Adobe Walls was a disaster for the tribesmen. Scattering, small bands went back to their usual tactics, raiding isolated farms and ranches and attacking small groups of hunters on open ground along the Texas, Oklahoma, and Kansas frontiers.

THE FINAL CAMPAIGN

As a result of the Adobe Walls battle, in August 1874, the army demanded that some of the Penatekas who were camping on the Oklahoma reservation surrender their rifles and other weapons. Refusing, the Comanches fled the reservation and retreated to their last redoubts on the Llano Estacado in the Texas Panhandle. The army, determined to break Comanche and Kiowa resistance in what became known as the Red River War, sent a three-pronged assault force equipped with Gatling guns and howitzers to round up the tribes and herd them back to the reservation.

On September 12, three companies of the 8th US Cavalry sighted a large band of Comanche and Kiowa warriors near Sweetwater Creek, a branch of the Red River. As the troopers charged, the warriors retreated, keeping up a running fire as they fled to the northeast.

The band, under a Kiowa war chief named Lone Wolf, lured the troopers away from the Indian women and children hiding behind a high ridge. At the sound of gunfire, the Kiowa non-combatants packed up their camp and fled southwest. Under a boiling Panhandle sun, in what was to be called the Battle of Sweetwater Creek, the warriors fled for miles down the creek until they finally eluded their pursuers.

Meanwhile, the aged Spotted Pony, in company with another mixed band of Comanches and Kiowas, attacked and laid siege to a wagon train bringing supplies to the army. After three days of pinning down the circled wagons and failing to overrun the teamsters' defenses, the Indians abandoned the siege.

While retreating south to rejoin their families, on September 12, Spotted Pony and more than 100 warriors spotted four soldiers and two civilian scouts. The men were carrying dispatches to Colonel Nelson Miles, commanding the 6th Cavalry Regiment.

Screaming their war cries, the Comanches charged and began to circle their foes. The soldiers dismounted and, falling prone, opened up a rapid fire. A soldier holding their mounts was shot dead and the horses stampeded. As the fight continued, all but one of the whites, the scout Billy Dixon, were wounded. Dixon spotted a shallow depression in the ground called a buffalo wallow. Limping and staggering, the five men managed to get to the wallow. There they kept

In 1870, hunters began a massive slaughter of the buffalo herds. They sold the animals' hides to eastern merchants; the meat, source of life to the Comanches, was left to rot on the prairie. (Texas State Library)

up a sufficient fire to keep the warriors from overrunning them, but their situation was desperate. Later that afternoon, however, a severe storm poured down stinging rain. At that, the warriors abandoned the fight and rode south to rendezvous with the main body of their tribe.

"It is a good day to die"

The last major battle of the Red River War began on September 27, 1874, when Colonel Mackenzie's 4th Cavalry scouts located the Comanche–Kiowa camp hidden in Palo Duro Canyon. The canyon is a wild and haunted place. There the Prairie Dog Town Fork of the Red River has carved weird spires and pinnacles of rocks which cast fantastic shadows along the canyon floor. The winds rebounding off the steep canyon walls create shrieking sounds which the superstitious claim are the cries of those murdered along the banks of the Prairie Dog Town stream.

The canyon is a 120 mile (190km) finger pushing into the Llano Estacado plateau. Its rim stands 3,500 feet (1,070m) above sea level, and plunges more than 1,000 feet (300m) to the canyon floor. The canyon's walls sheltered both Indian camps and roaming buffalo from the freezing "northers" that roar down from the Canadian plains during winter. Good water was available from the Prairie Dog Town stream that ran along the canyon floor, and there was sufficient grass to feed thousands of buffalo or cattle.

At Mackenzie's encampment, the scouts reported seeing several thousand horses and long rows of tepees stretching along the stream. At the news, Mackenzie had his bugler blow "Boots and Saddles" and the 4th Cavalry swung into a swift 25 mile (40km) march toward the hostiles' camp.

At dawn, September 28, scouts found a trail leading to the canyon floor. When the troopers reached the bottom of the canyon, one company stampeded more than 1,000 Indian horses down the canyon while the main body of the regiment, bugles blaring, charged into the unsuspecting camp.

Surprised, and without their horses, the warriors fought on foot. Desperately they kept up a covering fire with their lever-action rifles, allowing their women and children to escape down the other end of the canyon. Falling back from the carbine fire of the cavalrymen, one of the warriors cried, "We are lost. We must surrender."

Spotted Pony, one of the few warriors who had kept his horse close to his tepee, screamed, "Never." Throwing down his carbine, he dashed to his tepee, picked up his lance, put on his feathered war bonnet, and mounted his mustang. Above the roar of the gunfire he shouted to his young Comanche warriors, "It is a good day to die."

Buffalo hides stacked for shipment in Dodge City, Kansas. Dodge City, a railroad town, was headquarters for many of the buffalo hunters. Within a decade, millions of the animals were killed and the buffalo faced extermination. (National Archives)

Spurring his mount to a gallop, his long white hair flowing in the breeze, his lance point decorated with many scalps, he charged the cavalry firing line. A young lieutenant, seeing the old chief bearing down on his position screaming a war cry, pointed his saber at Spotted Pony and yelled, "Volley fire." A dozen carbines fired in unison and Spotted Pony and his mount crashed to the canyon floor.

The old warrior, sprawled on the ground, waved his broken lance, mouthed a Comanche curse, and died. He was the last warrior to die in the last major battle the Comanches would ever fight.

It was all over in a few minutes. The remainder of the warriors scattered into the arroyos and small canyons, hiding in the Palo Duro's myriad defiles and rocky trails. Later, when darkness came, they searched for their wives and children.

In all, the cavalry had killed only four warriors and suffered less than a dozen casualties, but they had captured almost 1,500 horses. Mackenzie gave 500 of them to his Tonkawa scouts and shot the remainder. Then he ordered his men to burn all the tepees and camp goods, including the supply of food the Indians had stored to keep them from starving during the coming winter.

Scattered bands of Comanches and Kiowas wandered through the canyon for days evading cavalry patrols. But without horses, the buffalo gone, their provisions destroyed, and winter coming on, with the women and children whimpering from hunger and the chilling winds, the disheartened tribes began to straggle back to the Oklahoma reservations. Quanah Parker and 400 diehards held out for a while but surrendered in June 1875 at Fort Sill, Oklahoma. The Comanche wars were finally over.

For more than 150 years they had been the lords of the plains, but now they were reduced to making a meager living on a reservation by farming or ranching. A quarter of a century of poverty followed until, by 1901, there were only 1,000 members left of the haughty, fearless tribe of mounted warriors who had been the terror of the south west.

THE AFTERMATH

In ensuing years, conditions improved. A booming economy, good schools, and the high energy of the people eventually brought the Comanches into the modern age.

During World War II, warrior traditions were revived when young Comanches fought with courage alongside their fellow Americans. Members of the tribe served in all branches of the armed forces.

On June 6, 1944, when Allied troops landed in Normandy, 13 Comanche soldiers in the 4th Infantry Division, 4th Signal Company, waded ashore onto Utah Beach. Setting up field radios, they transmitted artillery instructions from regimental headquarters to division headquarters in the Comanche language. One of the first messages off the beach was sent by Private Charles Chibitty requesting reinforcements: "Five miles to the right of the designated area and five miles inland the fighting is fierce and we need help."

While some of the Comanche code-talkers were wounded in action, all of them survived the war. Theirs was a code the Wehrmacht never deciphered. The code-talkers thoroughly confounded German intelligence and their secure channel of communications is credited with saving the lives of countless Americans and Allies. By war's end they had been heavily decorated by both American and Allied commanders.

Texans regularly celebrate and re-enact the battles of the Alamo and San Jacinto, but they have never observed the Council House Fight, Plum Creek, or Palo Duro. There was too much terror and bitterness for

The Plains Indians launched numerous attacks against the buffalo hunters but were unable to stop the 5,000 hunters destroying their way of life. As the buffalo were slaughtered, farmers moved in to plow the plains, and ranchers replaced the buffalo with herds of cattle to graze on the sea of grass. (Denver Public Library)

the participants and their children's children to want to remember. And later generations have mostly forgotten the frontier times and the fierce battles that raged across the plains.

Today there are more than 10,000 Comanches, most of them living in southwest Oklahoma. Their number includes prosperous doctors, lawyers, farmers, ranchers, and not a few merchant chiefs.

GLOSSARY

adobe	sun-dried mud brick
Anglo	Mexican and Indian term for Europeans other than Spaniards
Comanche moon	full moon in late summer or early fall
Comancheros	New Mexican merchants who traded with Comanches
counting coup	landing a blow or touching an enemy in hand-to-hand combat
corral	enclosure for confining livestock
empresarios	land agents who were commissioned to bring emigrants onto Spanish/Mexican lands
gringos	Americans or Europeans
lariat or **lasso**	a rope of leather with a running noose
Llano Estacado	(or **Staked Plains**) open grassy plains in northwest and southwest Texas
mustang	small, hardy horses that roamed wild on the western plains. They were descended from escaped or captured Spanish horses
presidio fort	a fortified outpost in hostile Indian country
Pueblo Indians	New Mexico tribes that were settled and peaceful agriculturalists
puta	spiritual power
remuda	herd of horses
tepee	Comanche tent
Texican	European Texan
vision quest	search for spiritual power

BIBLIOGRAPHY

DeShields, James T., *Border Wars of Texas*, State House Press, Austin, 1933 (first published 1912)

Fehrenbach, T.R., *Comanches: The Destruction of a People*, Alfred A. Knopf, New York, 1974

Haley, James L., *The Buffalo War*, University of Oklahoma Press, Norman, 1976

Jenkins, John Holland, *Recollections of Early Texas: The Memoirs of John Holland Jenkins*, University of Texas Press, Austin, 1958

Newcomb, William W. Jr., *The Indians of Texas*, University of Texas Press, Austin, 1961

Nye, W.S., *Carbine and Lance: The Story of Old Fort Sill*, University of Oklahoma Press, Norman, 1937

Richardson, Rupert Norval, *The Comanche Barrier to the South Plains Settlement*, A.H. Clark Co., Glendale, 1933

Smithwick, Noah, *Evolution of a State*, Gammel Book Co., Austin, 1900

Thrall, Homer S., *A Pictorial History of Texas*, N.D. Thompson & Co., St. Louis, 1879

Wilbarger, J. W., *Indian Depredations in Texas*, Eakin Press, Austin, 1985 (first published 1889)

The brutal ending of a buffalo hunter caught by Comanches near Dodge City in 1868. The warriors fought men like him with fury and desperation. Buffalo hides brought the hunters $3.75 apiece and many hunters, killing 250 animals a day, got rich (if, of course, they were able to keep their scalps intact). (National Archives)

COLOR PLATE COMMENTARY

A: COMANCHE WARRIOR (1830)

By 1700 the Comanches had mastered the horse and begun their conquest of the Southern Plains. Short, stocky people, they adapted their clothing and weapons to their hunting and raiding culture.

During the hunting, horse stealing, and raiding seasons from the late spring to late fall, and particularly during the hot months on the Texas plains, the warriors stripped for action, wearing little more than doeskin breechcloths and calf-high leggings of buckskin. Their moccasins were sewn with buffalo hide.

Their straight black hair was parted in the middle, twisted into braids which streamed down each side of the warrior's head. A warrior left a long scalp lock in the middle of his hair in which turkey or buzzard feathers were often tied.

The weapons used for fighting, except for the shield, were also used for hunting.

(1) The short bow was designed for use on horseback.

(2) A dozen or more arrows were carried in a leather scabbard slung over the shoulder.

(3) The wooden lance could be 8 to 14 feet (2.4–4.3m) long. In the early days the point was fire-hardened wood or a sharpened piece of flint attached to the end of the pole. Later, Comanches used steel points traded from New Mexicans.

(4) For close fighting the warriors relied on a war club with a flexible leather handle of twisted buffalo hide and a stone war head.

(5) Also used for close fighting were steel tomahawks first acquired from French traders and later from Comancheros.

(6) Every Comanche warrior carried a steel scalping knife. These knives were short-bladed and very sharp.

(7) Comanche shields were formed into a circle from springy bent branches over which tough buffalo hide was stretched. The hide was often stuffed with hardened leather and pushed out into a convex outer shape to present a rounded surface to better turn arrows or lance points. Often they were garishly painted. From the center of the shield the warriors tied buffalo tails or, preferably, scalps. For the latter, blonde hair was especially favored.

B: CAMP LIFE

Whenever possible, Comanches made camp along a flowing stream. Horses were picketed downstream from the tepees. During the winter months the tepee was the preferred dwelling for the tribe. Easy to put up, take down, and transport, the average tepee was constructed with a framework of 16 to 22 poles and was usually more than 15 feet (4.6m) high.

Tanned buffalo hides were sewn together and wrapped around the poles from the ground to about 14 feet (4.3m) high, giving an interior 12 to 16 feet (3.5–5m) in diameter. A flap at the top allowed smoke from a fire to be vented.

Deer skins and buffalo robes kept the Comanches snug in cold and rainy weather. Traders maintained that in snow and freezing winds the tepee was warmer and more comfortable than the drafty log cabins of the white settlers.

Comanche camps were temporary affairs, and in the warm months they were packed up when the tribe followed the buffalo herds. The Comanches usually made a semi-permanent camp to wait out the winter months.

During the day, the women gathered berries and plants and worked at scraping and stretching hides for making dresses, shirts, and containers. They were also in charge of gathering firewood, butchering buffalo, cooking food, taking care of children, and packing goods when the camp moved. Girls worked alongside their mothers.

The life of a Comanche woman was hard, but that of a white woman captive was a living hell. Mrs Rachel Plummer was pregnant when captured at Fort Parker, Texas, in May 1836 and held prisoner for 18 months until she escaped.

During that time she gave birth to a son. When the child's crying annoyed one of the warriors, he tied a rope around the baby's neck, mounted his horse, tied the other end of the rope to his saddle, spurred his horse and galloped in a circle. Rachel recounted, "My little innocent was not only killed but torn to pieces … they threw the remains of my child into my lap, and I dug a hole in the earth and buried him."

Repeatedly beaten, Rachel recounted, "I suffered more than I ever had done in my life." In the winter when there was snow on the ground, "I seldom had any covering for my feet and but very little clothing for my body."

While the women worked, the warriors, when not hunting or raiding, loafed or played games – often shooting dice for hides or knives – racing horses, or bragging about their exploits in scalping or counting coup.

Mow-way or Shaking Hand, chief of the Kwahadis, and 200 other Comanches were hiding in the Texas Panhandle in September 1872 when they were attacked by 4th Cavalry Buffalo Soldiers (black cavalrymen). The soldiers killed 50 warriors, captured 130 women and children, and burned the camp. (National Archives)

When the camp was to be moved, tepees were taken down and permanent supplies were loaded onto pack horses or on travois. A travois consisted of two tepee poles serving as shafts between a platform of hides upon which camp goods were piled. The whole contraption was then hitched to a horse. When horses were scarce, some of the Comanches' numerous camp dogs were put to work hauling the travois.

C: THE BUFFALO HUNT

The wild galloping buffalo hunts taught the Comanches hard lessons in horsemanship, archery, and the use of the lance.

The American buffalo or bison was huge. A full-grown bull, for example, was 7 feet (2m) tall at the shoulder and could weigh more than a ton. With no natural enemies, the buffalo bred and multiplied on the grassy plains until they were estimated to number more than 50 million.

Fortunately for the hunter, the buffalo were sluggish, stupid, and easily panicked. The favorite method of hunting was for groups of 30 to 40 mounted men to partially surround a herd and then, whooping and hollering, stampede it. Galloping down on the herd, they rode within 30 yards (30m) of the frenzied animals and launched their arrows so as to pierce the area behind the buffalo's short ribs. The wounded animal soon dropped.

Stronger, more experienced warriors demonstrated their prowess by hunting with the lance. If this was more exciting, it was also more dangerous. Riding close to the charging beast, the hunter used both hands to drive his lance point into the buffalo's neck or back, hoping the maddened beast would not hook his horns into his horse's flank or into the rider's thigh.

A lunging buffalo colliding with a horse could bring down horse and rider in a bone-cracking fall made lethal if the buffalo's massive body fell on top of its assailants. There were other dangers too. A racing horse could easily plant a hoof in a prairie dog hole, fall, and pitch its rider into a dangerous spill. A stampeding herd could also lurch into an unlucky horse and rider caught in its path and trample them under the weight of hundreds of the frightened beasts.

But the glory was worth the risks. After the women had butchered the beasts where they fell and loaded meat and hides onto a travois, the proud warriors led their caravan back to camp singing proudly of their prowess. A feast would follow.

D: VISION QUEST

Our young protagonist, who was still using his child's name when he reached the age of 15 or 16 years old, began to prepare himself for the most important event in his life – to seek and find his vision.

Before he could become a full-fledged warrior and join a raiding party the Comanche boy must first seek his puta or spiritual power. This vision quest was the search for the supernatural force that would guide his destiny and give him strength and protection.

When the boy believed he was ready to seek his puta, the band's medicine man or spiritual guide spoke to him of Comanche beliefs and supervised the purifying baths he would undergo. Then, stripped to his breechcloth and shrouded with a buffalo robe, the boy wandered from camp, searching for a secluded place where he could meditate in isolation. At intervals he stopped and smoked tobacco from his stone pipe and prayed to the great spirit.

Reaching his secluded "ashram," he fasted and prayed during the four-day retreat, hallucinating from hunger, thirst, and intense meditation, as he searched for a vision. When it arrived, he saw vaporous images of animals, heard songs carried on the wind, and then visualized the taboos and charms that would guide his life.

One night, sleeping on a high ridge overlooking a deep canyon, the boy was awakened by a blasting clap of thunder. Groggy and dazed, he looked into a star-studded sky, ripped by great bolts of lightening. Then he saw it.

Enveloped in a gray cloud he saw a Comanche chief in a full-feathered war bonnet riding a spotted pony which was running freely across a sepulchral plain. The chief carried a lance from which many scalps were tied. His shield and his deerskin-fringed shirt and pants were snow white. The galloping pony was also snow white with several brown and black spots on its rump. The vision was very grayish, hazy, and vaporous – but it was the boy's sign. It was his puta. His child's name was forgotten and he took the warrior's name of Spotted Pony.

During the 1870s the Comanches again fielded superior weapons when they purchased lever-action rifles from the Comancheros. The cavalry was armed with old single-shot Springfields. (Denver Public Library)

Armed with his new puta and mystical guardian, he returned to the camp where he was accepted into the ranks of the warriors and welcomed into the raiding parties. From that time on Spotted Pony would gain stature as an accomplished horse thief and a deadly killer of Comanche enemies which included Apaches, Mexicans and, particularly, Texans.

E: TRADING WITH THE COMANCHEROS

By 1786 the Comanches had learned the advantages of steel weapons and implements and had agreed to a truce between themselves and the Spanish/Mexican merchants of

Below: A Kiowa warrior who rode with the Comanches drew this picture of the Battle of Buffalo Wallow, in which warriors attacked four troopers of the 6th Cavalry and two civilian scouts. One private was killed and others wounded. (Texas Memorial Museum, University of Texas at Austin)

New Mexico. The warriors agreed not to raid Spanish settlements in return for the right to trade horses and loot seized from the Pueblo Indians and Mexicans in exchange for steel knives, lance points, arrowheads, tomahawks, kettles, and assorted trinkets.

The treaty with the Spaniards protected the thriving settlements of Santa Fe and Taos from the murderous raids launched at settlements in Texas and northern Mexico. In exchange for the freedom to go unmolested and trade in New Mexico, the Comanches aided the Spaniards in their attacks on the Apache war bands which were devastating smaller New Mexican towns and haciendas.

As Spanish power declined and their Mexican successors held only a tenuous authority over the Southern Plains, many of the smaller towns paid tribute to Comanche war bands to preserve the peace and avoid being pillaged. Comanche chiefs openly boasted that they allowed Mexican towns to exist only to provide them with steel implements and to raise good horses that they could steal.

In later years, Mexicans traded rifles and pistols for ransomed captured fellow countrymen, and Texan and American women and children. Also popular as trading goods were gaudy European fabrics and bolts of colored cloth, which the Comanches made into clothes and saddle blankets.

Below: The decisive battle of the Comanche wars was fought in Palo Duro Canyon, where a large encampment of Comanches and Kiowas was attacked by the cavalry. The warriors were scattered and the tribes never again fought a major battle with the army. (The University of Texas Institute of Texas Cultures at San Antonio)

When the American Civil War ended and the US Cavalry began to re-establish forts on the Southern Plains, New Mexican traders loaded their wagons and drove out into Comancheria country. They became the only persons allowed in Comanche camps unmolested. These traders, known as Comancheros, kept up a lively trade in gun-running until the tribe's power was crushed.

F: ATTACK ON THE WAGONS

On a morning in the late summer of 1838, James Webster handed his little daughter up to his wife who was already seated on their wagon. He waved to the 12 men on the other three wagons and then climbed onto the driver's seat. Webster cracked his bull hide whip and the four horses hitched to the wagon lurched forward. The other three wagons followed.

Webster was moving his family north from Austin to pioneer his new land grant in Williamson County in central Texas. As they plodded along the trail, they were spotted by a war band of Comanches who silently trailed behind them.

To the Comanches, the white men were interlopers who would steal their land, kill their buffalo, and hunt down and murder their people. Of all the enemies who invaded their lands, the Texans were the worst.

When evening came, Comanche scouts watched the white men form the wagons into a hollow square and tie the hobbled horses to a picket line. There were 16 horses to steal, 13 men to kill and scalp and, best of all, there was a blonde white woman and small girl who would be useful to ransom or to serve as camp slaves.

That night the war band planned their attack, then slept until an hour before dawn. The warriors painted their bodies with vertical red stripes. Some painted their foreheads black while others daubed white or yellow stripes down the bridge of their noses. They mounted their horses in the darkness and silently rode toward the camp.

At first light they observed drowsy men preparing a breakfast fire. Then the Comanche leader let out a piercing scream and the band, 40 strong, charged down on the camp. As the white men leaped into the wagons and reached for their rifles the warriors loosed a fusillade of arrows.

Some of the whites were killed instantly. The survivors opened fire at the Comanches who, screaming war cries, galloped around the circled wagons. The Texans' single-shot rifles were slow to reload and completely ineffective against the Comanches – for every shot fired by the Texans, the raiders loosed 20 arrows. One by one the settlers dropped, some looking like human pincushions with multiple arrow wounds. When the Texans' fire slackened, the Comanches plunged toward the wagons and used their lances to deliver the coup de grace to any survivors.

ABOVE LEFT **Chief Isa Rosa or White Wolf, chief of the Yamparika Comanches, was considered by the Americans to be one of the most treacherous leaders of the tribe. He said, "I would rather eat dung than live on a reservation." (National Archives)**

Defeated and disillusioned after they were forced onto reservation land, many Comanches turned to the drug peyote. Led by Shamans (LEFT), peyote rituals gave the warriors visions and a feeling of contentment. (Denver Public Library)

Both the dying and the dead were scalped. Mrs Webster and her daughter were found huddled on the floor of the lead wagon. The war band took the prisoners, piled valuables onto the captured horses, set the wagons ablaze and rode off to the north. They celebrated the destruction of another group of white settlers who would never profane Comanche lands.

Mrs Webster and her daughter were held captive for almost two years until they escaped the Comanche camp while the men were off on a raiding trip. The two managed to make their way to San Antonio.

G: THE BATTLE OF PLUM CREEK

In early August 1840, the Comanches banded together for a massive raid into south Texas. Led by their war chief Buffalo Hump, an estimated 700 braves, accompanied by women and children, slipped from their camps in the Texas hill country.

On August 5, they were spotted by several Texans who quickly spread the word of the approaching war party. At 4.00pm the next afternoon under a boiling Texas sun, the Comanches charged into the town of Victoria. Shooting and burning, they killed 13 settlers and drove off a herd of more than 1,000 horses and mules.

Continuing southward they killed more settlers, stole more livestock, and burned more homes until at dawn on August 8 they reached the bustling port of Linnville on the Gulf Coast. Screaming war cries, they galloped into the town shooting arrows and spearing the unsuspecting residents.

Most of the settlers escaped by running into the Gulf waters and swimming to ships anchored off shore.

The raiders looted the town and began to burn it. Before the fires spread, however, they plundered a waterfront warehouse stocked with European clothes and laughingly slipped these over their breechcloths. A Linnville survivor reported that several braves perched black silk top hats over the turkey feathers in their hair. One brave donned a frock coat backward, buttoning it from behind. Breaking into a box of parasols, the Comanches opened them out and, holding them high, rode triumphantly through the burning town. Some took bolts of colored ribbon and tied them to their horses' tails. That night, as the town burned, they began a leisurely ride north.

Other Texas settlers had not been idle since the Comanches were first spotted. As the word of the raid spread, rifles were taken from mantelpieces and horses were saddled. Volunteers assembled while scouts spread out across the prairies to track the Comanche retreat. Studying the terrain, Texas Rangers and local militia planned to get ahead of the raiders and cut them off at Plum Creek, near the present city of Lockhart.

On the morning of August 12, more than 200 Texans took positions in chaparral lining a wide swath of open prairie. Their alignment resembled a hollow square, open in front. Concealed in the brush, they waited patiently.

Soon, arrogant and careless, the Comanche caravan came into view singing and whooping. It was a bizarre column of strangely dressed braves, milling horses, and mounted women captives clutching their small children. Comanche women brought up the rear leading mules loaded with plunder.

When they got within range the Texans opened fire. It started a wild stampede as the Comanches whipped their horses into a frenzied retreat. After the first fusillade the Texans mounted and gave chase in a running fight for more than 15 miles (25km).

As they retreated, the Comanches slew all their prisoners except for one woman, dumping their bodies in the path of the pursuing Texans. Abandoning much of their loot when the horses carrying it gave out, the raiders escaped to their hill country hideouts.

They left behind the bodies of 50 dead warriors. During the battle one Texan was killed and seven wounded. More than 30 settlers had been killed.

Most of the Comanches escaped, but this was no Indian victory. The Comanches never again posed a major threat to settlers in south and central Texas. For the next 35 years there were only minor raids on isolated farm and ranch houses in that part of Texas.

H: COMANCHE WARRIOR (1874)

In the years following the American Civil War, the US Cavalry re-entered the Southern Plains with the purpose of breaking Comanche power. Each cavalryman was armed with a

For many years the warriors, deprived of the old ways, were unable to become integrated into the modern world. For these "lords of the plains," life on the reservation was not only one of poverty, but for "The finest light cavalry in the world," it was also boring. Finally, however, prosperity slowly returned as the Comanches learned to farm and ranch. (National Archives)

single-shot Springfield carbine that was deadly at 500 yards (450m), as well as a single-action Colt six-shot revolver.

The warriors now realized that the traditional Comanche weapons were no longer superior to those of their enemies. Determined to attain superior firepower, they chose to outshoot the cavalrymen by purchasing from Comancheros and renegade American gun-runners the rapid-fire 1860 model Henry carbine or the 1866 Winchester carbine. Both were lever-action, short-barreled repeating rifles which, although they lacked the range of the Springfields, could fire faster than the army's single-shot breechloaders.

With magazines carrying 11 to 14 rounds, the short-barreled carbines could be rapidly fired by a lever which pumped the bullets into the breech as fast as the trigger could be pulled and the lever arm worked. The short length of the carbines enabled them to be fired accurately by the expert Comanche horsemen.

In a mounted engagement at medium ranges they had the advantage of firepower over the cavalry, whose Colt revolvers were designed for short range shooting and were highly inaccurate at more than 75 yards (70m).

The Comanches further improved their weaponry when they purchased a number of the new Winchester Model 1873 lever-action carbine which carried 11 cartridges in its magazine. An added advantage was that the new Frontier Model Colt revolver was chambered for the same 44.40 cartridge used by the carbine. This meant that the same ammunition, when obtained could be used in revolver and carbine, a great help to a people who were always short of ammunition for their rifles. Some Comanche warriors began to favor Texan-type Bowie knives while others sported older US and Mexican army bayonets that had been sold for surplus, captured or discarded by those services.

During the 1870s many of the tribesmen favored the full-feathered war bonnet and most continued to wear the traditional deerskin shirt, trousers, and leggings which offered protection from the brush and cacti found on the plains. Some warriors wore a breastplate of white bones held together by rawhide strips decorated with brass beads.

Unfortunately for the tribe, repeatedly famished as the buffalo disappeared and badly outnumbered by the cavalry, their dwindling ranks of warriors could not prevail against the surge of white civilization.

These Comanche code-talkers trained at Fort Benning, Georgia, before they were sent overseas to Great Britain. On D-Day, June 6, 1944, they were among the first to land during the invasion of Normandy. (National Archives)

INDEX

References to illustrations are shown in **bold**. Plates are shown with page and caption locators in brackets.

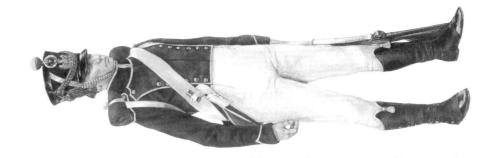 

FIND OUT MORE ABOUT OSPREY

❏ Please send me the latest listing of Osprey's publications

❏ I would like to subscribe to Osprey's e-mail newsletter

Title / rank _____

Name _____

Address _____

_____

City / county _____

Postcode / zip _____ state / country _____

e-mail _____

I am interested in:

❏ Ancient world
❏ Medieval world
❏ 16th century
❏ 17th century
❏ 18th century
❏ Napoleonic
❏ 19th century

❏ American Civil War
❏ World War 1
❏ World War 2
❏ Modern warfare
❏ Military aviation
❏ Naval warfare

Please send to:

USA & Canada:
Osprey Direct USA, c/o MBI Publishing, P.O. Box 1, 729 Prospect Avenue, Osceola, WI 54020

UK, Europe and rest of world:
Osprey Direct UK, P.O. Box 140, Wellingborough, Northants, NN8 2FA, United Kingdom

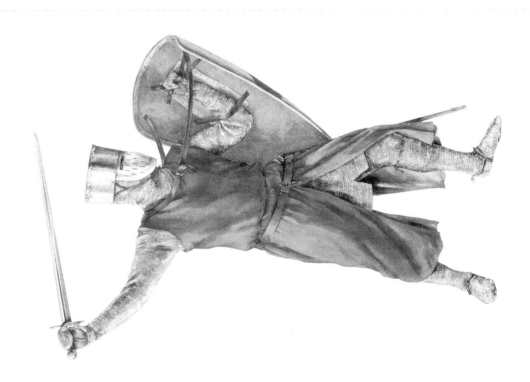

OSPREY
PUBLISHING

www.ospreypublishing.com

call our telephone hotline
for a free information pack

USA & Canada: 1-800-826-6600
UK, Europe and rest of world call:
+44 (0) 1933 443 863

Young Guardsman
Figure taken from *Warrior 22:
Imperial Guardsman 1799– 1815*
Published by Osprey
Illustrated by Christa Hook

Knight, c.1190
Figure taken from Warrior 1: Norman Knight 950– 1204 AD
Published by Osprey
Illustrated by Christa Hook

POSTCARD